...tablished
...el brands,
... in travel.

...years our
guidebooks have unlocked the secrets
of destinations around the world,
...ing with travellers a wealth of
...rience and a passion for travel.

Rely on Thomas Cook as your
... companion on your next trip
...efit from our unique heritage.

Thomas Cook **pocket** guides

MOSCOW

Your travelling companion since 1873

Thomas Cook

Written by Marc Di Duca
Updated by Oleg Polikarpov

Published by Thomas Cook Publishing
A division of Thomas Cook Tour Operations Limited
Company registration No: 3772199 England
The Thomas Cook Business Park, 9 Coningsby Road
Peterborough PE3 8SB, United Kingdom
Email: books@thomascook.com, Tel: +44 (0)1733 416477
www.thomascookpublishing.com

Produced by The Content Works Ltd
Aston Court, Kingsmead Business Park, Frederick Place
High Wycombe, Bucks HP11 1LA
www.thecontentworks.com

Series design based on an original concept by Studio 183 Limited

ISBN: 978-1-84848-301-9

Series Editor: Kelly Pipes
Production/DTP: Steven Collins

Printed and bound in Spain by GraphyCems

Cover photography (St. Basil's Cathedral) © Jon Arnold Images/Alamy

CONTENTS

SYMBOLS KEY

The following symbols are used throughout this book:

address telephone website address email
opening times public transport connections important

The following symbols are used on the maps:

airport	points of interest
hospital	city
police station	large town
railway station	small town
metro	motorway
cathedral	main road
numbers denote featured cafés & restaurants	minor road
	railway

Hotels and restaurants are graded by approximate price as follows:
£ budget price **££** mid-range price **£££** expensive

Abbreviations used in this guide are:

bul.	bulvar (boulevard)	pl.	ploschad (square)
nab.	naberezhnaya (river bank)	pr.	prospekt (avenue)
per.	pereulok (side street)	ul.	ulitsa (street)

Note that Russian addresses often have both a street number and a building number. 'Klimentovsky per. 10/2', for example, means Klimentovsky Street no. 10, building no. 2.

A riverboat cruises down the Moskva River past the Kremlin

INTRODUCING
Moscow

Introduction

The crisp winter sun glancing off a gilt onion dome; the commanding walls of the secretive Kremlin; stern-faced soldiers stomping across Red Square; a ballerina executing effortless pirouettes on the stage of the Bolshoi Theatre – these are images that come to mind when one hears the name Moscow. This is the unique capital of a huge nation, the epicentre of all things Russian: sometimes extravagant, brash, and eager to show off its new-found wealth; at other times stylish, understated, cosy and highbrow. No longer the grey headquarters of the Communist world, bustling, multicultural Moscow has it all. So throw off any stereotyped preconceptions and immerse yourself in Slavdom's biggest and most exciting metropolis.

The city has undergone a transformation in the last decade, from poverty-stricken centre point of a failing state to proud, fast-moving and ever more affluent capital of a risen nation. Whether it's vibrant nightlife, high culture, the fascinating Communist legacy or historical grandeur you are looking for, Moscow provides it in socialist-era portions. Dance the night away at an extravagant nightclub, dress up for an evening at the ballet, tuck into some filling Russian fare at one of the city's hundreds of restaurants, relax in Gorky Park or feel history all around you on Red Square. Moscow is always on the move, a place that bombards the senses with its grand architecture, incense-filled churches and booming traffic.

While Moscow may be known as one of the most expensive cities in the world, it's easy to visit without breaking the bank. Besides, admission charges to Moscow's tourist sights are still low by Western standards and tickets for the ballet or a concert are much cheaper than in the West.

Though Moscow may present challenges – monster roads, unresponsive waiters, double-pricing and the like – if you move with the rhythm of the city and overlook its minor irritations, then this, one of the greatest cities in the world, becomes inspiring, uplifting and fascinating.

Moscow illuminated

When to go

There's no one single time of the year you should or shouldn't head for the Russian capital. Of course, some months are better than others, but all have their charms. The city has a completely different face in every season of the year; so don't think Moscow is automatically at its best in summer, as the winter snow, the blossom-coated spring and the hazy autumn are romantic and colourful times to be in the city.

Firework celebrations in Moscow for New Year

SEASONS & CLIMATE

Moscow 'enjoys' an extreme continental climate, meaning sweltering summers and bitterly cold winters with lots of snow. The typical winter temperature is -10°C (14°F). In summer the mercury usually hovers around 25°C (77°F). These are typical values, so don't be surprised when temperatures dive to -30°C (-22°F) in January and rocket up to 35°C (95°F) in July. Spring and autumn are much more comfortable, though early spring can be a muddy affair.

ANNUAL EVENTS

January

Orthodox Christmas (7 Jan) More of a family affair than a raucous street party – Muscovites make special Christmas dishes and attend church. If you are in Moscow at this time, you might only notice the streets becoming a bit quieter.

February

Maslenitsa Shrovetide (over one week from 28 Feb 2011; 20 Feb 2012; 11 Mar 2013) Carnival to you and me – just don't expect skimpy costumes and samba in the streets as the temperature can still be well below zero. To mark the beginning of Lent, Russians eat pancakes and, in a classic case of a Christian festival laced with pagan ritual, the end of winter is celebrated by casting a straw witch (representing winter) into the river.

March

International Women's Day (8 Mar) Some call it a kind of Soviet Valentine's Day, others see it as a good excuse for a day off work and a booze up.

March & April

Golden Mask Festival This festival of performing arts takes place at various venues around Moscow and in other Russian cities. It culminates in a lavish award ceremony. Ⓦ www.goldenmask.ru

April

Easter Sunday (24 Apr 2011; 15 Apr 2012; 4 May 2013) Easter according to the Russian Orthodox calendar falls later than in the Catholic or Protestant churches. Midnight mass is held, special food prepared and a festival of classical and choir music takes place in the city's churches.

May

May Day (1 & 2 May) May Day is not the grand sabre-rattling event it once was and is now just the first in a series of days off in early May. Many people make a 'bridge' between the 2nd and 9th, meaning some shops and offices are closed for almost half of May.

Victory Day (9 May) Marks what is interpreted as Communism's martial triumph over Nazism in 1945 (see page 12).

June & July

Moscow Film Festival The Russian capital's biggest film event, with screenings all over town. Ⓦ www.moscowfilmfestival.ru

September

Moscow City Day On the first weekend of September the city – quite rightly – celebrates itself (see page 12).

October

Kremlin Cup Moscow's annual tennis thwack-and-grunt fest held at the Olympic Stadium. ⓦ www.kremlincup.ru

December

Russian Winter Art Festival Three weeks of icy fun in the freeze-dried Moscow air, including an ice sculpture competition on Red Square and swimming in the Moskva River. Other events and activities take place at the Izmaylovo Park between mid-December and early January.

New Year The last night of the year across the Russian-speaking world is the equivalent of Christmas in the West (25 December is a normal working day in Russia). Russians typically gorge on a special salad called *Olivier* (potato, carrot, egg, chicken, gherkin and mayonnaise), caviar sandwiches, citrus fruits and champagne. Towards midnight everyone heads for the city centre to watch a firework display and crack open the Sovyetskoe champers.

PUBLIC HOLIDAYS

New Year's Day 1 Jan
Eastern Orthodox Christmas 7 Jan
Defender of the Fatherland Day 23 Feb
International Women's Day 8 Mar
International Labour Day/May Day 1 May
Victory Day 9 May
Independence Day 12 June
National Unity Day 4 Nov

Moscow's red letter days

Every year, Moscow sees two big red letter days, the like of which you simply won't experience anywhere else.

Known in Britain as Victory in Europe Day (though celebrated throughout Europe on 8 May), Victory Day (9 May), or *Den Pobyedy* as the Russians call it, marks the triumph of the USSR over Nazi Germany in 1945. Around a week before the day itself, Red Square (see page 65) is cordoned off, huge decorations bearing countless hammers and sickles are suspended across streets, and Muscovites tie orange-and-black pieces of striped ribbon (the ribbon of St George, a potent symbol of military honour in Russia) onto car aerials, lampposts and even around their heads. Unfortunately, on the day itself you need a ticket to see the military parade and pop concert on Red Square, but there are other processions to keep the visitor entertained. A long Communist Party procession bearing portraits of Lenin and Stalin makes its way nostalgically towards the Lubyanka (see page 82), and the military are out in force, too. Moving about the city centre can be a headache as roadblocks prevent anyone from getting near the Kremlin (see page 66) and Red Square, and the Garden Ring Road is closed.

Floats on Tverskaya Street, a historical fair and general festivities, concerts, street performances and much drinking in every park and square in the city centre make City Day (6 September, or the nearest Saturday), or *Den Goroda*, a much jollier affair than Victory Day, and this is one you really shouldn't miss if you want to make friends with the locals. As it's held on a Saturday, the celebrations usually spill over into Sunday.

Victory Day street decorations

History

Prince Yury Dolgoruky is regarded as the founder of Moscow. It was he who built the first fortress (the original Kremlin) on this strategic site at the marshy confluence of the Moskva and Yauza rivers. Initially a small community ruled by the nearby Vladimir-Suzdal principality, by the 13th century, Moscow, becoming ever richer on trade, was an independent city state.

Led by Genghis Khan's grandson, Batu, the Mongols swept their way across the Eurasian steppe, destroying everything in their path. Reaching Moscow in 1237, they all but razed it to the ground. For the next 200 years, Moscow laboured under the Mongol yoke (though the yoke was seriously weakened when Dmitry Donskoy defeated them at Kulikovo in 1380). Despite this, the city's power grew under Ivan the Great, who eventually rid Muscovy of the Mongols in 1480. The state continued to expand under Ivan the Terrible in the 16th century. In 1571, the Mongols returned, this time in the form of the Crimean Tatars, who reduced the city to smouldering ash.

In 1712, Tsar Peter the Great, never a fan of Moscow, upped sticks and started afresh in purpose-built St Petersburg. Decline soon followed in Moscow and, by 1725, its population had decreased by 25 per cent.

In 1812, Napoleon invaded Russia and in September his forces confronted the Tsar's army at Borodino, 130 km (80 miles) outside Moscow. Napoleon took the city without a fight, though most of the population had fled and torched the city before they left. Napoleon declared victory, but only one French soldier in 20 returned home, many falling victim to the cruel Russian winter.

Dissatisfaction with the Tsar and social conditions across Russia led to the 1917 Revolution. Unrest began in St Petersburg and quickly spread to Moscow, which was reinstated as capital by Lenin. Stalin took over after Lenin's death in 1924 and set about destroying many of Moscow's medieval churches and other historical buildings. When Hitler invaded Russia in 1941, the Russian winter once again came to the people's aid and Moscow was never taken by the Nazis.

Post-war Communism could hardly be said to have been a huge success on many levels. After decades of paranoia, human rights abuses and a failing economy, Mikhail Gorbachev and Boris Yeltsin called time on the Soviet Union in 1991. Throughout the 1990s, unchecked capitalism replaced state control and the economy went into freefall. Conflict between President Yeltsin and the Parliament led to bloodshed in 1993, and currency devaluation in 1998 caused further upheaval. However, when Vladimir Putin assumed office as president in 2000, Moscow began to become increasingly stable and rich, though at the expense of some civil liberties and the Kremlin's relationship with the West. Putin has since been succeeded as president by Dmitry Medvedev, but remains a powerful political figure in the form of prime minister.

Tomb of the Unknown Soldier with the Eternal Flame

Lifestyle

Moscow boasts over 30 resident billionaires. Armani suits and Cartier watches sell here by the truckload, and Bentleys are snapped up like hot *bliny*. But, of course, for most of the 10.5 million people who call Moscow home such luxury is a distant dream. The average monthly wage in Moscow is just under $400 (£200), though from the cars on the streets and the price of goods in the shops you'd never guess. Head out from the Garden Ring Road in any direction and you'll soon arrive at miles and miles of high-rise concrete blocks where the vast majority of Muscovites dwell and where the Russians' relative poverty is more obvious. If we are to believe the hype, Russia is now an oil-rich country where a Mercedes broods in every driveway, but one trip to the end of any metro line will convince you otherwise.

Most Muscovites lead pretty humdrum lives, commuting to work on the crowded metro in the morning, dealing with the stresses of work all day, then fighting their way home again in the evening to be fed a diet of pop music, variety shows and mild propaganda on TV. Life is expensive, and there's injustice, corruption and inequality all around them, but most shut this out, taking comfort from family life, children, country cottages (known as *dachas*), hobbies and nature. Although most people live on grim Soviet-era housing estates, there's still a stronger sense of community than in the West and neighbours still look out for one another.

Of course, many have done well for themselves under the new system, and at no time in Russian history have young people had so many opportunities to study, do business and make dreams come true. Many lead hectic lives, studying, holding down several jobs, building a dacha outside Moscow, while bringing up kids and looking after elderly relatives. Moscow flats are usually on the small side but then so are Russian families. Very often grandparents live with their children as there is very little social care available from the state. Much of family life takes place around the kitchen table in the evening, when the various members gather to eat and chat.

Although religion has made a big comeback across Russia since the collapse of the Soviet Union, it tends to be the old (women) who take an active role. Moscow is possibly the most liberal and hedonistic city in Russia, but views on homosexuality, race and gender tend to be very conservative. Politically, Russia has gone back to a more authoritarian system, which seems to suit most Russians if it guarantees security and stability. People are generally very satisfied with the way the ruling party, United Russia, runs the country – or at least that's what they'll tell you.

Muscovites commute to work through an ornate metro system

Culture

As you would expect from a major city and the focus of the Russian-speaking world, Moscow has a wealth of culture unrivalled in Eastern Europe. There are enough museums, galleries, concert halls and theatres to provide a lifetime of experiences, and highbrow culture is one of the strongest cards Moscow has to play when it comes to attracting visitors.

Anyone who's anyone in Russian cultural history has lived, worked and sometimes died in the capital. Gogol, Bulgakov, Chekhov, Mayakovsky, Pushkin, Tolstoy, Lermontov and Dostoyevsky (as well as countless artists and composers) all lived here. Many of their flats and houses have been preserved exactly as they left them as house museums (see page 100).

Moscow is a mecca for fans of classical music, opera and ballet. What could be better than experiencing Tchaikovsky's *Nutcracker* or *Swan Lake* at the Bolshoi Theatre (see page 85) or enjoying some Shostakovich at the Tchaikovsky Concert Hall (see page 98)? Other world-class performance venues to check out are the State Kremlin Palace (see page 71) and the New Opera (see page 101). If you say you don't like ballet and claim that classical music is boring, Moscow is the city that will change your mind.

Unless you speak Russian, most theatre is off the menu, but occasionally the **Moskovskii Khudozhestvennyi Teatr Imeni A. Chekhova** (Chekhov Moscow Art Theatre ⓐ Kamergersky per. 3 ⓣ (495) 692 6748 ⓦ www.mxat.ru Ⓜ Metro: Teatralnaya or

The Bolshoi Theatre

Plenty of classical concerts add to the highbrow culture scene in Moscow

Okhotny Ryad) puts on English versions of classic Russian plays. Unfortunately for those arriving in Moscow in the summer months, most venues close between late June and September, when conductors, musicians and actors retreat to their dachas for some hard-earned R&R.

For information on buying tickets for cultural events, see page 33.

Moscow's river winds past Gorky Park and the Kremlin

MAKING THE MOST OF
Moscow

Shopping

The very idea of travelling to Russia a decade or two ago to shop would have been absurd. The minimal selection of pickles, vodka and clumsy electrical goods to be found gathering dust on the shelves of dour state-run shops did not exactly constitute an exciting retail experience. Times have certainly changed since the mean days of Communism, and now everything you could possibly need, want and desire (and a great deal you don't) is available in Moscow's exclusive emporia and huge cathedrals of choice. Price has replaced availability as the main obstacle to a happy shopping experience, and the cost of many items (especially luxury goods) you can buy back home has been pumped up considerably for a market obsessed with expense at all cost! There are few bargains to be had in the Russian capital though that is not true of Russia as a whole.

As far as souvenirs are concerned, the archetypal gift is the Russian nesting doll (*matryoshka*), usually a gaudily painted series of dolls, one fitting perfectly inside the next. Some are made to resemble the Russian president Medvedev or prime minister Putin, and there are even dolls of Barack Obama. Lacquered boxes, spoons, ladles and plates in black, red and gold make attractive gifts, as do boxes, coasters and even shoes made of birch bark. Many street stalls sell Soviet memorabilia such as medals, badges, posters, chunky military watches and Red Army equipment such as binoculars and canteens, though much of what you find today is made in China. Retro poster

Moscow has plenty of modern shopping centres

The well-known *matryoshka* dolls of Russia make great souvenirs

USEFUL SHOPPING PHRASES

How much is...?
Сколько стоит...?
Skol-ka sto-it...?

Can I try this on?
Можно примерить?
Mozh-na prim-ye-rit?

I'm a size...
Мой размер...
Moy raz-myer...

I'll take this one
Возьму
Vaz-mu

reproductions cost thousands of roubles but the real period pieces fetch a hundred times more. The days when you could pick up a valuable antique at a flea market are long gone, and Russian sellers are now very much aware of the value of items. Be aware that exporting an authentic antique made before 1960 requires a licence. Religious icons, samovars, fur hats, caviar, pirate CDs and DVDs and of course souvenir bottles of vodka are other items that weigh down visitors' suitcases on their way back to Sheremetyevo Airport (see page 48).

Although outside the areas covered by this guide, the sprawling **Izmaylovo Market** (W www.kremlin-izmailovo.com ⏲ 09.00–18.00 Sat & Sun Ⓜ Metro: Partizanskaya or Cherkizovskaya) known locally as Vernisage and located around 9 km (5½ miles) east of Red Square, is the best source of good value souvenirs in the capital.

Eating & drinking

Those who believe Russian food to be a bland procession of pickles and overcooked cabbage are in for a pleasant surprise: Russian cuisine throws up some very tasty dishes. The country has partially adopted the cuisine of its former 'colonies', and Georgian and Central Asian dishes provide some welcome spice. As a major city, Moscow has a plethora of international restaurants serving up curries, sushi and pasta for very high prices.

Russian *zavtrak* (breakfast) can seem odd, with many tucking into leftovers from the previous day's dinner. Traditional Russian breakfast fare includes *bliny* (pancakes), *kasha* (porridge) and *tvarog* (cottage cheese), washed down with a cup of black tea without milk. The working day begins later in Russia and *obed* (lunch) is usually eaten between 13.00 and 15.00. Once the main meal of the day, this is now often a hurried snack. That said, most restaurants serve a so-called 'business lunch', a relatively inexpensive three-course set menu. The evening *uzhin* (meal) will be a modest affair of *zakuski* (snacks) such as pancakes with sweet and savoury toppings, *salat* (salad), salted fish, cold meats and occasionally sandwiches topped with (now quite expensive) *ikra* (red caviar).

PRICE CATEGORIES

Prices are per person, for an average three-course meal, excluding wine.

£ up to 400RUR **££** 400–1,000RUR **£££** over 1,000RUR

Russian cuisine is based on peasant staples such as *borsch* (beetroot soup), *myaso* (meat), *pelmeni* (ravioli filled with meat served with a dollop of sour cream), *ukha* (fish soup), *shchi* (cabbage

Borsch *is one of the most common dishes in Russia*

soup), *griby* (mushrooms) in countless forms and *ryba* (fish). Main courses come with potatoes, vegetables, pasta, salad or rice. Popular ethnic dishes include *shashliki* (kebabs) from Georgia, *plov* (pilau rice) from Uzbekistan, *holubtsi* (cabbage rolls stuffed with seasoned rice) from Ukraine, *chebureki* (savoury pastries) from Central Asia and *tolma* (stuffed vine leaves) from Armenia. Desserts are sometimes disappointing, with *morozhenoe* (ice cream), *pirogi* (pies), pancakes with sweet toppings and *baklava* (sweet pastry) ever-present.

Vegetarians can get by quite easily, and if you eat fish, you're laughing. Pancakes, porridges, vegetable *plov* (rice) and some soups are just a few of the dishes vegetarians can enjoy. (As across all of Eastern Europe, watch out for hidden ham.)

Russians are up there at the top of the league when it comes to tea consumption. *Chai*, as tea is known in numerous Eurasian languages, is served black with sugar, lemon and cheese or biscuits. *Kofe* (coffee) is still a rather hit-and-miss affair and you may be gasping for a proper triple espresso by the time you head back to Sheremetyevo Airport. All the usual culprits of the fizzy-drink world are widely available but the traditional Russian soft drinks are *kompot*, a sugary squash made with berries and other fruit, and *kvas*, a thirst-quenching concoction produced from fermented bread.

Although vodka is still imbibed in liver-pickling amounts, French and Armenian cognacs have taken over as the prestigious moonshines of choice. Russian *pivo* (beer) is of excellent quality but *vino* (wine) is still to be avoided away from upmarket restaurants.

Dining at Moscow's restaurants can be expensive, so save

USEFUL DINING PHRASES

I would like a table for two
Я бы хотел столик на двоих
Ya bih khat-yel sto-lik na dvoikh

Could I have the bill, please?
Счёт, пожалуйста?
Shot, pa-zhal-sta

Waiter!
Официант!
A-fit-sih-ant!

It is meat free?
Зто без мяса?
E-ta byez mya-sa?

Where is the toilet?
Где туалет?
G-dye tu-al-yet?

money by eating in cafés or ethnic restaurants, or by taking advantage of cheaper business lunches. Self-catering is another option, but do note that grocery stores are also fairly overpriced. Most restaurants now have menus in English – although if you are given one in Cyrillic, that's all part of the fun!

Entertainment & nightlife

Moscow offers the full range of clubs and bars, from grungy student dives to techno palaces and laid-back hippy joints to full-blown strip clubs. Some of the more foreigner-friendly places double up as cheap cafés during the day with chairs and tables shoved to one side for dancing in the evening. These usually have very long and even 24-hour opening times. The more mainstream places are packed with the young, rich and beautiful of Moscow's scene or not so beautiful gangs of Russian teenagers. Vodka-fuelled fist fights and worse are common in discos. Of course, the elite frequent a completely different world of exclusive clubs with very strict entry rules. With the exception of alternative and student hangouts, almost all nightclubs have so-called face control enforced by the ugliest, meanest bouncers you are ever likely to come across. Don't mess with these characters – if they say 'no trainers', they mean 'no trainers'. There's a strip club and unofficial brothel on almost every street in Moscow city centre, often frequented by Western businessmen on expense accounts and Russian wannabe oligarchs.

The classic pub concept is alien to Russians, and many bars double up as cafés, clubs etc. A couple of Bavarian-style beer halls have popped up in recent years, but British and Irish pubs have yet to make an impact.

In the world of cinema, *The Battleship Potemkin*, shot in 1925, remains the best-known Russian film. If you understand Russian, some of the Soviet comedies from the 1960s to the mid-1980s are great entertainment, but after that low-quality Hollywood blockbuster-style movies took over. If you're determined to see

Moscow is a centre for classical music

Catch an evening performance at the Bolshoi Theatre

TICKETS & TOUTS

Tickets for the Bolshoi Theatre (see page 85) should be bought as early as possible from the website, the box office or a tout (haggle the price down, if you're feeling confident). For all other venues, you should contact the box office direct. Seeing a performance is still inexpensive by Western standards, though the day of the dirt-cheap ticket is over.

a Russian-made film, seek out Nikita Mikhalkov's Oscar-winning *Burnt by the Sun* as well as his other films *The Barber of Siberia* (in English), *12* and *Territory of Love*. The other name to look out for is Andrei Zviagintsev, who received two Venice Golden Lions for his film *The Return*. The vast majority of films are dubbed into Russian, so a visit to the cinema in Moscow may not be the best night's entertainment. Try the **Dome Cinema** (ⓐ Renaissance Moscow Hotel, Olimpisky pr. 18/1 ⓣ (495) 931 9873 ⓦ www.domecinema.ru Ⓜ Metro: Prospekt Mira), where pictures are often shown with their original soundtrack intact.

Russian pop music is in fairly bad shape, with Soviet-era singers Alla Poughatcheva, Sofia Rotaru, Valeri Leontiev remaining popular among the older generation. Younger people prefer hip-hop artists such as Timaty or Casta, and rock and pop stars including Dima Bilan, Valeria, Mummi Troll and Zemfira. A better option for music lovers is jazz, which was banned by the Communist authorities for being too American but is becoming increasingly popular now. There are several worthy jazz clubs dotted around the city centre.

Sport & relaxation

SPECTATOR SPORTS

Russia's two national sports are football and ice hockey. Not surprisingly, Moscow has five football teams in the top division of the Russian football league – **Dynamo** (ⓦ www.fcdynamo.ru), **CSKA** (ⓦ www.pfc-cska.com), **Spartak** (ⓦ www.spartak.com), **Lokomotiv** (ⓦ www.fclm.ru) and **FC Moskva** (ⓦ www.fcmoscow.ru) – and three in the top flight in ice hockey: **Dynamo** (ⓦ www.dynamo.ru), **Spartak** (ⓦ www.spartak.ru) and **CSKA** (ⓦ www.cska-hockey.ru). Russia's extremely successful national ice hockey team are the current reigning champions, having won the 2008 and 2009 Ice Hockey World Championships. While crowd trouble at ice hockey is unheard of, hooliganism at football matches is still a major headache.

Moscow also hosts an annual tennis event, the Kremlin Cup (see page 11) held at the **Olimpiysky** (Olympic Stadium ⓐ Olympiysky pr. 16 ⓣ (495) 688 5322 ⓦ www.olimpik.ru ⓜ Metro: Prospekt Mira).

PARTICIPATION SPORTS

The Russian capital is not the ideal place to enjoy outdoor sporting activities, with perhaps the exception of skating in winter, tennis at one of the city's numerous clubs or jogging in Gorky Park or along the Moskva River embankment. Indoors, bowling has arrived in Eastern Europe and is a much more popular night out here than in the West. Billiards has also found a huge following though only some halls have classic American pool, and British snooker is a mystery to the Russians. The Russian version of billiards has completely different rules.

If you are trained up enough, Victory Day and City Day (see page 12) see marathons beginning and ending in Gorky Park. Due to the lethal nature of Moscow's roads, the insanity of Russian drivers and the complete absence of cycle tracks, you are strongly advised not to cycle in Moscow. For swimming, head to the pool at the Luzhniki complex, which was built for the 1980 Olympics.

Luzhniki complex ⓐ Luzhnetskaya nab. 24 ⓣ (495) 637 0764 or (495) 785 9717 ⓦ www.luzhniki.ru ◷ 07.00–22.00 Ⓜ Metro: Sportivnaya

RELAXATION

One of the best ways to relax in the Russian capital is to take to the *banya*, something akin to a sauna. The most famous in the city centre is the Sandunovsky Baths (see page 84).

Ice hockey practice in the Krylatskoe Ice Stadium

Accommodation

Accommodation is likely to be your greatest expense (and headache) when staying in the Russian capital. Such wonders as boutique hotels and old-world charm are virtually non-existent in Moscow and, all in all, visitors are faced with a choice between cramped but convivial hostels, sad Soviet hotels from hell or overpriced luxury.

There are few bargains out there, and anything of a decent standard comes with a hefty room rate, but for those on a budget there are several backpacker hostels in the city centre. One step up from these are the slightly drab Soviet-era hotels. From this category it is an enormous leap to the ever-increasing number of Western-style luxury 4- and 5-star chain hotels.

You are advised to find accommodation as near to the city centre as possible, preferably near a metro station. New Year is the only time when it's difficult to find a room/bed. Asking to see the room before you commit may be a good idea, and if reception staff refuse, go elsewhere. Reception staff come grumpy as standard, as do the security guards who patrol almost every accommodation facility in the city.

You can avoid all or most of the above by renting an apartment. Agencies have many to choose from and they are particularly

PRICE CATEGORIES

Prices are for double rooms, per night, not including breakfast.

£ up to 6,000RUR **££** 6,000–10,000RUR

£££ over 10,000RUR

good value for money if you are travelling with family or a group of friends.

HOTELS

Warsaw Hotel ££ Not much from the outside, but fully renovated inside and low room rates considering the central location near Gorky Park. Ⓐ Leninsky pr. 2/1 (Red Square, Kremlin, Kitay-Gorod & Zamoskvareche) Ⓣ (499) 238 4101 Ⓔ warsaw@sovintel.ru Ⓜ Metro: Oktyabrskaya

Arbat Hotel ££–£££ The rooms at this rather kitschy, Soviet-era hotel are still good value, well-maintained and relatively quiet despite the central location just 200 m (220 yards) off popular Arbat Street. Ⓐ Plotnikov per. 12 (Zemlyanoy Gorod) Ⓣ (495) 244 7628 Ⓜ Metro: Smolenskaya

East-West Hotel £££ Housed in a 19th-century mansion, this small hotel has bags of charmingly kitschy character and marries historical interiors with modern facilities. The central location on Tverskoy Boulevard is also a big plus. Ⓐ Tverskoy bul. 14/4 (Beliy Gorod) Ⓣ (495) 232 2857 Ⓦ www.eastwesthotel.ru Ⓜ Metro: Tverskaya

Metropol £££ Moscow's finest art nouveau building is simply breathtaking, inside and out. With its genuinely opulent 5-star luxury, this is one of the finest places to stay in town, and just a short hop from Red Square. Ⓐ Teatralny proezd 1/4 (Red Square, Kremlin, Kitay-Gorod & Zamoskvareche) Ⓣ (499) 501 7800 Ⓦ www.metropol-moscow.ru Ⓜ Metro: Teatralnaya

Radisson Royal £££ Occupying one of the Stalinist-era Seven Sisters skyscrapers, this Moscow institution was built in the 1950s and has recently been revamped by the Radisson group. Views across the Moskva River are incredible. ⓐ Kutuzovsky pr. 2/1 (Zemlyanoy Gorod) ⓣ (495) 933 6801 ⓦ www.radisson-hotels.ru Metro: Kievskaya

The splendid Radisson Royal, one of the famed Seven Sisters

APARTMENTS

Apartment Reservation Network This reliable company manages a portfolio of affordable, safe flats all renovated to Western standards. t (495) 225 5012 w www.apartmentres.com

Apartments Moscow Online and telephone bookings for apartments in central Moscow. t (495) 956 4422 w www.apartmentsmoscow.com

HOSTELS

Comrade Hostel £ Another great backpacker hang-out boasting contemporary interior design in a historical building in the Kitay-Gorod. a Maroseyka ul. 11, 3rd Floor (Red Square, Kremlin, Kitay-Gorod & Zamoskvareche) t (495) 628 3126 w www.comradehostel.com Metro: Kitay-Gorod

Napoleon Hostel £ Conveniently situated within the Kitay-Gorod, five minutes' walk east of Red Square, this is arguably Moscow's best hostel and deserves its rave reviews. Heaps of free stuff, full visa support and registration and a welcoming atmosphere. a Maly Zlatoustinsky per. 2, 4th Floor (Red Square, Kremlin, Kitay-Gorod & Zamoskvareche) t (495) 628 6695 w www.napoleonhostel.com Metro: Kitay-Gorod

Trans-Siberian Hostel £ A well-located hostel within walking distance of Kitay-Gorod and Red Square. Dorms can be a little cramped but there's a well-equipped kitchen and the staff are entertaining. No curfew. a Barashevskiy per. 12 (Zemlyanoy Gorod) t (495) 916 2030 w www.tshostel.com Metro: Kurskaya

THE BEST OF MOSCOW

Whether you're spending just a few hours in Moscow between planes or planning to stay a week, here are some aspects of this great city you should definitely not miss.

TOP 10 ATTRACTIONS

- **Red Square and the Kremlin** The very heart of this vast country, and dripping with symbols of Russian statehood (see pages 65 & 66)

- **The Arbat** Sip a beer or take an amble along Moscow's most happening street (see page 92)

- **A night at the Bolshoi Theatre** Catch a performance of *The Nutcracker* or *Swan Lake* at this iconic Moscow venue (see page 85)

- **Moscow's metro stations** Take a tour of the subterranean palaces that form the city's richly decorated, if slightly OTT, metro system (see pages 46 & 53–6)

- **Have a blast in a *banya*** Explore the feel-good possibilities of being lightly steamed, dipped in ice and flayed with twigs in a Russian bath house (see page 84)
- **The State Tretyakov Gallery** Two galleries, 100,000 works, one unforgettable experience (see page 72)
- **GUM** Now more Burberry than Bolshevik, the old state shopping centre is a temple to the luxury retail experience (see page 74)
- **A lazy afternoon in Gorky Park** Follow the Moskva down to Gorky Park to listen to that wind of change (see page 65)
- **St Basil's Cathedral** Moscow's flamboyant cathedral supports the most famous set of onion domes in the world (see page 71)
- **Georgian cuisine** Sample some fiery fare from this hot-blooded former Soviet Republic (see page 26)

Busy city streets near Red Square

Suggested itineraries

HALF-DAY: MOSCOW IN A HURRY

Many do find themselves leaving the confines of Sheremetyevo Airport (see page 48) with enough time on their hands between planes to spend a morning or afternoon in the city centre. With so little time, you'll be limited to the sights of the Kremlin and Red Square (see pages 65 & 66), and even then you won't be lingering long over anything.

1 DAY: TIME TO SEE A LITTLE MORE

The Kremlin and Red Square should be first on anyone's itinerary, and if you want to make the most of everything on offer here, that takes care of the hours of daylight. In the evening, take a relaxing stroll along the Arbat (see page 92) to watch the street performers, stopping at one of the cheap Russian eateries along the way or ending the evening with a spicy experience... in a Georgian restaurant, that is.

2–3 DAYS: TIME TO SEE MUCH MORE

The extra time means that you can properly absorb the nuances of the combined Kremlin and Red Square experience (see above) without rushing around and spoiling your dinner. The luxury of a second day means culture vultures can revel in the delights of the State Tretyakov Gallery (see page 72) and make an evening performance at the Bolshoi Theatre (see page 85), with perhaps a spot of luxury brand-name shopping at GUM (see page 74) in between. Enjoy an after-show dinner at a fine Russian restaurant such as Godunov (see page 77) or Café Pushkin (see page 89).

Plenty to see in the Kremlin

Spend day three relaxing in Gorky Park (see page 65), before rummaging for souvenirs at the Izmaylovo Market (see page 25), then take a subterranean tour of the wonderfully ornate metro system (see pages 46 & 53–6). End your visit with a night out at one of the city's extravagant nightspots.

LONGER: ENJOYING MOSCOW TO THE FULL

Four days or more means you can get off the beaten track, take a day trip to Suzdal (see page 106) or Sergiev Posad (see page 118), let off steam at the Sandunovsky Baths (see page 84), wonder at the size of the Seven Sisters skyscrapers (see page 97) and the Cathedral of Christ the Saviour (see page 78), then sample all the gastronomic delights Moscow's restaurants can throw at you, from haute-russe to Azeri and hot Georgian to exotic Uzbek fare.

Something for nothing

For a city that's famous around the world for being expensive to visit, Moscow has a surprisingly large amount to see and do that won't cost you a single kopeck piece. Red Square (see page 65), the many parks and gardens and the Moskva River embankments are all open spaces that can all be enjoyed at no cost. Moscow's churches are always open and, with some infamous exceptions, never charge admission (though the resident beggars outside each one may relieve you of a small fortune in change). Perhaps surprisingly, the Cathedral of Christ the Saviour (see page 78) won't cost you a *sosiska* (sausage) to inspect, either. As long as you don't actually buy anything, GUM (see page 74) can be considered a freebie, as can all the other shopping centres.

The 30 seconds you are allowed in Lenin's Mausoleum (see page 67) can be enjoyed without a rouble to your name, as can the Sakharov Museum (see page 101), and the Matryoshka Museum (see page 131). On 18 May, International Museums Day, museums waive their admission fees, and on 16 May, Museums Night, museums open their doors free of charge during the late evening. **Svyato Danilov** (St Daniel's Monastery ⓐ Danilovsky Val 22 ⓣ (495) 958 0502 ⓦ www.msdm.ru), the headquarters of the Russian Orthodox Church in the south of the city, also allows visitors to browse its churches, chapels and the Trinity Cathedral for free.

A popular activity for the financially challenged is touring Moscow's metro system, which is so cheap to ride, it may as well be free. Markets are another pleasure that won't cost you anything to browse, though Moscow's best market, the Izmaylovo (see

GUM... the most famous department store in Russia

page 25), does charge a nominal 10RUR to deter pickpockets. Strolling the Arbat, lazing on the grass in Gorky Park (see page 65), practising your unintelligible Russian on innocent passers-by and admiring the views across the city from Universitetskaya ploschad are further activities that don't require you to know your PIN.

When it rains

Rain may pose a temporary inconvenience at any time of year, but in winter, when the mercury plummets and the vertical snow rasps hands and faces, it may be keeping warm rather than dry that concerns you most.

Taking shelter in one of the city's many museums and galleries is the obvious choice when the heavens open or your nose begins to freeze. The State Tretyakov Gallery (see page 72) can keep you busy for days if you choose, and others, such as the State Historical Museum (see page 71) and the Pushkin Museum of Fine Arts (see page 85), are also superb places to improve the mind and the temperature of the body.

Diving into one of Moscow's many churches is always a wet-weather option, although they are not the best locations if you want to sit out the gloom as Orthodox places of worship have no pews! However, the decorative glories within will soon banish any thoughts of a nice sit down. If you can dodge the raindrops in between buildings, then the Kremlin (see page 66) is also feasible.

In the winter months the musty warmth of Moscow's metro system is welcome relief from the cold, and a tour of the most extravagantly decorated stations is a great way to kill half a day. The most eye-popping stations to head for are Kievskaya, Mayakovskaya, Ploshchad Revolyutsii, Novoslobodskaya, Novokuznetskaya, Prospekt Mira and Komsomolskaya, and almost all except the most recently built have some stunning artwork.

Naturally, shopping in one of the city's ever-increasing

number of indoor shopping centres such as the GUM (see page 74) will get you out of the cold, though the Muscovites' obsession with expense and luxury may limit you to window shopping only.

Rodin sculptures in the Pushkin Museum of Fine Arts

On arrival

TIME DIFFERENCE

Moscow Time is three hours ahead of GMT. Between the end of March and the end of October, clocks are put forward by one hour for Daylight Saving Time.

ARRIVING

By air

Moscow has five airports: **Bykovo** (t (495) 558 4933), **Domodedovo** (t (495) 933 6666 w www.domodedovo.ru), **Sheremetyevo 1 & 2** (t (495) 232 6565 w http://svo.aero) and **Vnukovo** (t (495) 937 5555 w www.vnukovo-airport.ru). The vast majority of flights from Western Europe and North America land at Sheremetyevo 2 and Domodedovo.

IF YOU GET LOST, TRY ...

Do you speak English?
Вы говоритє по-английски?
Vih ga-va-rit-ye pa-an-gli-ski?

Where is...?
Где...?
G-dye...?

Could you show me on the map?
Покажите мне, пожалуйста на карте?
Pa-ka-zhih-tye mnye, pa-zhal-sta na kart-ye?

To get from Domodedovo to the centre, catch the high-speed **Aeroexpress** train link (www.aeroexspress.ru), which takes around 40 minutes to reach Paveletsky Station south of the river. Alternatively you can take a *marshrutka* (shared minibus taxi) or bus to Domodedovskaya metro station. If you land at Sheremetyevo 2, you can take the Aeroexpress to Belorussky Station, a journey which takes around 35 minutes. *Marshrutkas* run from Sheremetyevo 2 to Rechnoi metro station at the end of line 2 or Planernaya Station, the final stop on line 7. The Aeroexpress also links Vnukovo airport to Kievsky Station.

If you decide to take a taxi instead, be sure to agree on a price before you commit.

By rail

Moscow has many railway stations, and the one at which you will arrive depends largely on where you have come from. Trans-Siberian passengers' first sight of Moscow will be **Yaroslavsky Vokzal** (Komsomolskaya pl. 5 (495) 921 5914) in the northeast of the city; travellers from the Caucasus generally step onto the platform of the nearby **Kazansky Vokzal** (Komsomolskaya pl. 2 (495) 266 3181); those travelling from St Petersburg arrive at **Leningradsky Vokzal** (Komsomolskaya pl. 3 (495) 262 9143), also nearby; visitors coming from Poland, Berlin, Belarus and Kaliningrad will disembark at **Belorussky Vokzal** (Tverskoy Zastavy pl. 7 (495) 251 6093) in the northwest. *Vokzal* means 'station' in Russian. Komsomolskaya metro station serves Yaroslavsky, Kazansky and Leningradsky, while Belorussky has its own metro station, Belorusskaya.

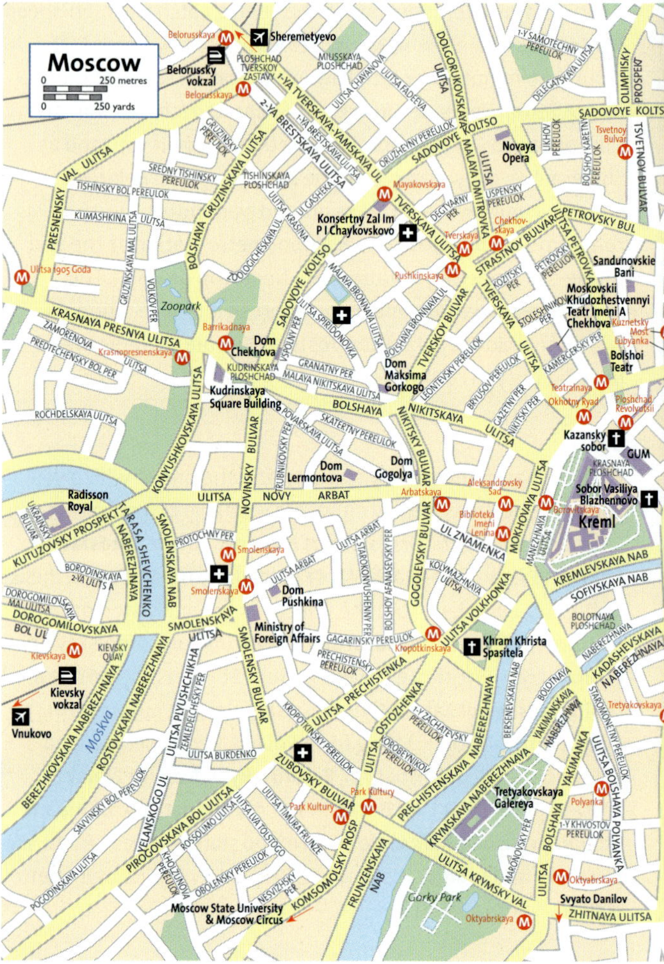
Moscow
0 250 metres
0 250 yards
Belorusskaya
Sheremetyevo
Belorussky vokzal
Ploshchad Tverskoy Zastavy
Miusskaya Ploshchad
1-ya Tverskaya-Yamskaya Ul
2-ya Brestskaya Ulitsa
Dolgorukovskaya Ulitsa
1-y Samotechny Pereulok
Delegatskaya Ulitsa
Olimpiisky Prospekt
Sadovoye Koltso
Tsvetnoy Bulvar
Tsvetnoy Bulvar
Novaya Opera
Malaya Dmitrovka Ulitsa
Gruzinsky Pereulok
Presnensky Val Ulitsa
Sredny Tishinsky Pereulok
Tishinsky Bol Pereulok
Tishinskaya Ploshchad
Bolshaya Gruzinskaya Ulitsa
Klimashkina Ulitsa
Gruzinskaya Mal Ulitsa
Mayakovskaya
Konsertny Zal Im P I Chaykovskovo
Tverskaya Ulitsa
Chekhovskaya
Tverskaya
Pushkinskaya
Petrovsky Bul
Ulitsa Petrovka
Strastnoy Bulvar
Sandunovskie Bani
Moskovskii Khudozhestvennyi Teatr Imeni A Chekhova
Kuznetsky Most
Lubyanka
Bolshoi Teatr
Ulitsa 1905 Goda
Zoopark
Krasnaya Presnya Ulitsa
Barrikadnaya
Dom Chekhova
Krasnopresnenskaya
Sadovoye Koltso
Kudrinskaya Ploshchad
Kudrinskaya Square Building
Granatny Per
Malaya Nikitskaya Ulitsa
Dom Maksima Gorkogo
Tverskoy Bulvar
Teatralnaya
Okhotny Ryad
Ploshchad Revolyutsii
Rochdelskaya Ulitsa
Bolshaya Nikitskaya Ulitsa
Kazansky sobor
GUM
Krasnaya Ploshchad
Konyushkovskaya Ulitsa
Novinsky Bulvar
Povarskaya Ulitsa
Dom Lermontova
Dom Gogolya
Nikitsky Bulvar
Aleksandrovsky Sad
Sobor Vasiliya Blazhennovo
Radisson Royal
Ulitsa Novy Arbat
Arbatskaya
Biblioteka Imeni Lenina
Borovitskaya
Kreml
Kutuzovsky Prospekt
Taras Shevchenko Naberezhnaya
Smolenskaya Nab
Smolenskaya
Ulitsa Arbat
Ul Znamenka
Mokhovaya Ulitsa
Kremlevskaya Nab
Sofiyskaya Nab
Dom Pushkina
Gogolevsky Bulvar
Dorogomilovskaya Bol Ul
Smolenskaya Ulitsa
Ministry of Foreign Affairs
Gagarinsky Pereulok
Kropotkinskaya
Ulitsa Volkhonka
Khram Khrista Spasitela
Bolotnaya Ploshchad
Kadashevskaya Naberezhnaya
Kievskaya
Kievsky Quay
Kievsky vokzal
Vnukovo
Prechistensky Pereulok
Ulitsa Prechistenka
Ulitsa Ostozhenka
Smolensky Bulvar
Ulitsa Plyushchikha
Tretyakovskaya
Berezhkovskaya Naberezhnaya
Moskva
Rostovskaya Naberezhnaya
Ulitsa Burdenko
Zubovsky Bulvar
Prechistenskaya Naberezhnaya
Bersenevskaya Nab
Yakimanskaya Naberezhnaya
Yakimanka
Polyanka
Ulitsa Bolshaya Polyanka
Park Kultury
Park Kultury
Tretyakovskaya Galereya
Krymskaya Naberezhnaya
Pirogovskaya Bol Ulitsa
Ulitsa Lva Tolstogo
Ulitsa Timura Frunze
Komsomolsky Prosp
Frunzenskaya Nab
Gorky Park
Ulitsa Krymsky Val
Oktyabrskaya
Oktyabrskaya
Svyato Danilov
Zhitnaya Ulitsa
Moscow State University & Moscow Circus

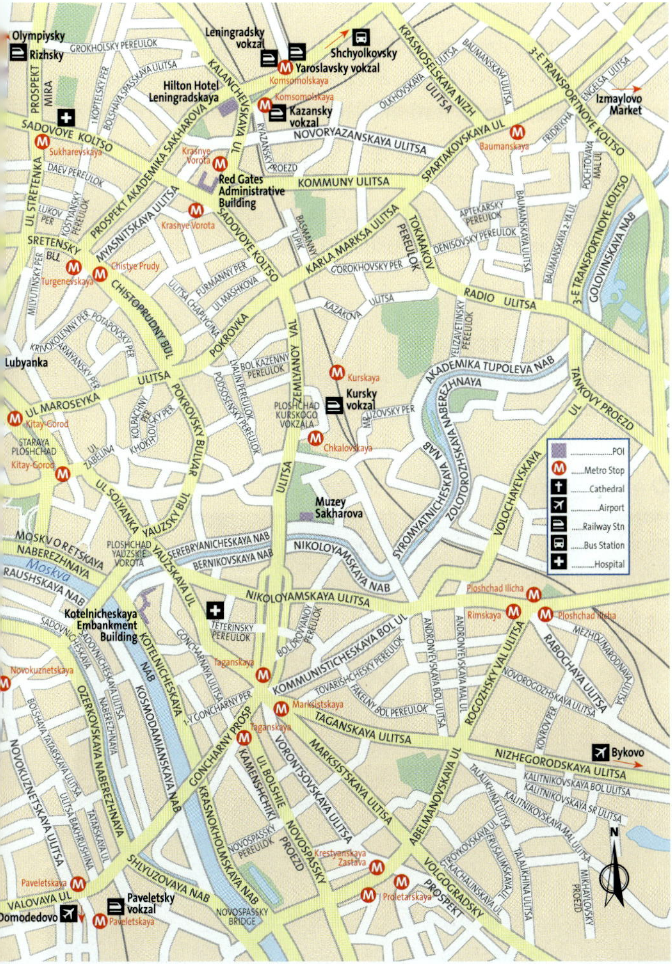

Olympiysky
Rizhsky
GROKHOLSKY PEREULOK
PROSPEKT MIRA
Leningradsky vokzal
Shchyolkovsky
Yaroslavsky vokzal
Komsomolskaya
Hilton Hotel Leningradskaya
Kazansky vokzal
KALANCHEVSKAYA UL
SADOVOYE KOLTSO
Sukharevskaya
DAEV PEREULOK
NOVORYAZANSKAYA ULITSA
KRASNOSELSKAYA NIZH ULITSA
3-E TRANSPORTNOYE KOLTSO
Izmaylovo Market
SPARTAKOVSKAYA UL
Baumanskaya
Krasnye Vorota
Red Gates Administrative Building
KOMMUNY ULITSA
PROSPEKT AKADEMIKA SAKHAROVA
MYASNITSKAYA ULITSA
UL STRETENKA
SRETENSKY BUL
Turgenevskaya
Chistye Prudy
CHISTOPRUDNY BUL
KARLA MARKSA ULITSA
TOKMAKOV PEREULOK
DENISOVSKY PEREULOK
RADIO ULITSA
GOLOVINSKAYA NAB
POKROVKA
ZEMLYANOY VAL
Kurskaya
Kursky vokzal
AKADEMIKA TUPOLEVA NAB
TANKOVY PROEZD
Lubyanka
UL MAROSEYKA
Kitay-Gorod
POKROVSKY BULVAR
Chkalovskaya
UL SOLYANKA
YAUZSKY BUL
Muzey Sakharova
VOLOCHAYEVSKAYA UL
MOSKVORETSKAYA NABEREZHNAYA
Moskva
RAUSHSKAYA NAB
SEREBRYANICHESKAYA NAB
NIKOLOYAMSKAYA NAB
NIKOLOYAMSKAYA ULITSA
Ploshchad Ilicha
Rimskaya
Kotelnicheskaya Embankment Building
KOTELNICHESKAYA NAB
Taganskaya
Novokuznetskaya
KOMMUNISTICHESKAYA BOL UL
ROGOZHSKY VAL ULITSA
Marksistskaya
TAGANSKAYA ULITSA
NIZHEGORODSKAYA ULITSA
Bykovo
GONCHARNY PROSP
KOSMODAMIANSKAYA NAB
OZERKOVSKAYA NABEREZHNAYA
NOVOKUZNETSKAYA ULITSA
MARKSISTSKAYA ULITSA
ABELMANOVSKAYA UL
KRASNOKHOLMSKAYA NAB
Krestyanskaya Zastava
Proletarskaya
VOLGOGRADSKY PROSPEKT
SHLYUZOVAYA NAB
Paveletskaya
VALOVAYA UL
Domodedovo
Paveletsky vokzal
NOVOSPASSKY BRIDGE
POI
Metro Stop
Cathedral
Airport
Railway Stn
Bus Station
Hospital
N

By road

Very few visitors arrive by road, though some may travel to Moscow on Ecolines coaches (see page 128) from Latvia. The Ecolines stop is outside the Rizhsky Station to the north of the city centre. If you are arriving from another city in Russia, chances are you'll end up at the long-distance Shchyolkovsky coach terminal 8 km (5 miles) to the east of the city centre, though your service may terminate somewhere else, usually in front of a railway or metro station.

FINDING YOUR FEET

Moscow can be a shock to the system at first, especially if you are arriving directly from the West. This is a fast-moving place

A metro train waits alongside the platform

where time and Muscovites wait for no man, especially not a tourist dithering at the metro doors or gazing nonplussed at a menu in a strange alphabet. Ease your way into Moscow – take it easy at a few quieter cathedrals or museums first before diving into the metro or swimming against the tide of tourists at the Kremlin (see page 66).

ORIENTATION

At the very core of the city are Red Square and the Kremlin (see pages 65 & 66), with the city radiating out from here in every direction. As the city spreads out it is divided into concentric rings by ring roads, starting with the Inner Ring Road, followed by the Boulevard Ring Road and the Garden Ring Road. South of the river are the Zamoskvareche District and Gorky Park (see page 65). With the exception of Kolomenskoye (see page 98), the areas beyond the Garden Ring Road are of little interest to tourists.

GETTING AROUND

The most user-friendly method of getting round Moscow is by metro. The system, which serves all parts of the city, is easy to use, cheap and runs from early morning until late at night. The system is huge and is used by more people per day than the London and New York undergrounds put together. Apart from the obvious rush-hour crowding issues, the only slight problem you may encounter is that all place names are, obviously, written in the Cyrillic alphabet, but even non-Russian speakers can usually decipher their destination. Maps with the Russian station names transcribed into English are also available. Buy tickets valid for multiple journeys to avoid having to queue every time.

Mitino МИТИНО 3
Volokolamskaya ВОЛОКОЛАМСКАЯ
Myakininskaya МЯКИНИНСКАЯ
Strogino СТРОГИНО
Krylatskoe КРЫЛАТСКОЕ
Molodezhnaya МОЛОДЕЖНАЯ
Kuntsevskaya КУНЦЕВСКАЯ 4
Pionerskaya ПИОНЕРСКАЯ
Filevsky Park ФИЛЕВСКИЙ ПАРК
Bagrationovskaya БАГРАТИОНОВСКАЯ
Fili ФИЛИ
Kutuzovskaya КУТУЗОВСКАЯ
7 Planernaya ПЛАНЕРНАЯ
Skhodnenskaya СХОДНЕНСКАЯ
Tushinskaya ТУШИНСКАЯ
Shchukinskaya ЩУКИНСКАЯ
Oktyabr'skoe Pole ОКТЯБРЬСКОЕ ПОЛЕ
Polezhaevskaya ПОЛЕЖАЕВСКАЯ
Begovaya БЕГОВАЯ
Ulitsa 1905 Goda УЛИЦА 1905 ГОДА
Krasnopresnenskaya КРАСНОПРЕСНЕНСКАЯ
Barrikadnaya БАРРИКАДНАЯ
Sheremetyevo ШЕРЕМЕТЬЕВО
Lobnya ЛОБНЯ
Rechnoy Vokzal РЕЧНОЙ ВОКЗАЛ 2
Voykovskaya ВОЙКОВСКАЯ
СОКОЛ Sokol
АЭРОПОРТ Aeroport
ДИНАМО Dinamo
Belorusskaya БЕЛОРУССКАЯ
Mayakovskaya МАЯКОВСКАЯ
Tverska ТВЕРСК
Pushkinsk ПУШКИНСК
Arbatska АРБАТСК
Mezhdunarodnaya МЕЖДУНАРОДНАЯ 4
Delovoy Tsentr ДЕЛОВОЙ ЦЕНТР
5
Kievskaya КИЕВСКАЯ
Smolenskaya СМОЛЕНСКАЯ
Arbatskaya АРБАТСКАЯ
Studencheskaya СТУДЕНЧЕСКАЯ
Kievskaya КИЕВСКАЯ
Smolenskaya СМОЛЕНСКАЯ
4
Aleksandrovsky Sad АЛЕКСАНДРОВСКИЙ САД
Park Pobedy ПАРК ПОБЕДЫ
Kievsky КИЕВСКИЙ
Slavyansky Bul'var СЛАВЯНСКИЙ БУЛЬВАР
Frunzenskaya ФРУНЗЕНСКАЯ
Park Kultury ПАРК КУЛЬТУРЫ
Biblioteka Imeni Lenina БИБЛИОТЕКА ИМ ЛЕНИНА
Vnukovo ВНУКОВО
Sportivnaya СПОРТИВНАЯ
Kropotkinskaya КРОПОТКИНСКАЯ
Vorob'evy Gory ВОРОБЕВЫ ГОРЫ
Universitet УНИВЕРСИТЕТ
Oktyabr'skaya ОКТЯБРЬСКАЯ
Prospekt Vernadskogo ПРОСПЕКТ ВЕРНАДСКОГО
Shabolovskaya ШАБОЛОВСКАЯ
Leninsky Prospekt ЛЕНИНСКИЙ ПРОСПЕКТ
Yugo-Zapadnaya ЮГО-ЗАПАДНАЯ 1
Profsoyuznaya ПРОФСОЮЗНАЯ
Akademicheskaya АКАДЕМИЧЕСКАЯ
Kaluzhskaya КАЛУЖСКАЯ
Novye Cheremushki НОВЫЕ ЧЕРЕМУШКИ
Belyaevo БЕЛЯЕВО
Kon'kovo КОНЬКОВО
Teply Stan ТЕПЛЫЙ СТАН
Sevastopol'skaya СЕВАСТОПОЛЬСКАЯ
Yasenevo ЯСЕНЕВО
10 Mar'ino МАРЬИНО Destination and Route
Interchange
Interchange (at street level 20-75 metres)
Chertanovskaya ЧЕРТАНОВСКАЯ
Bittsevsky Park БИТЦЕВСКИЙ ПАРК 6
9
Bul'var Dmitriya Donskogo БУЛЬВАР ДМИТРИЯ ДОНСКОГО

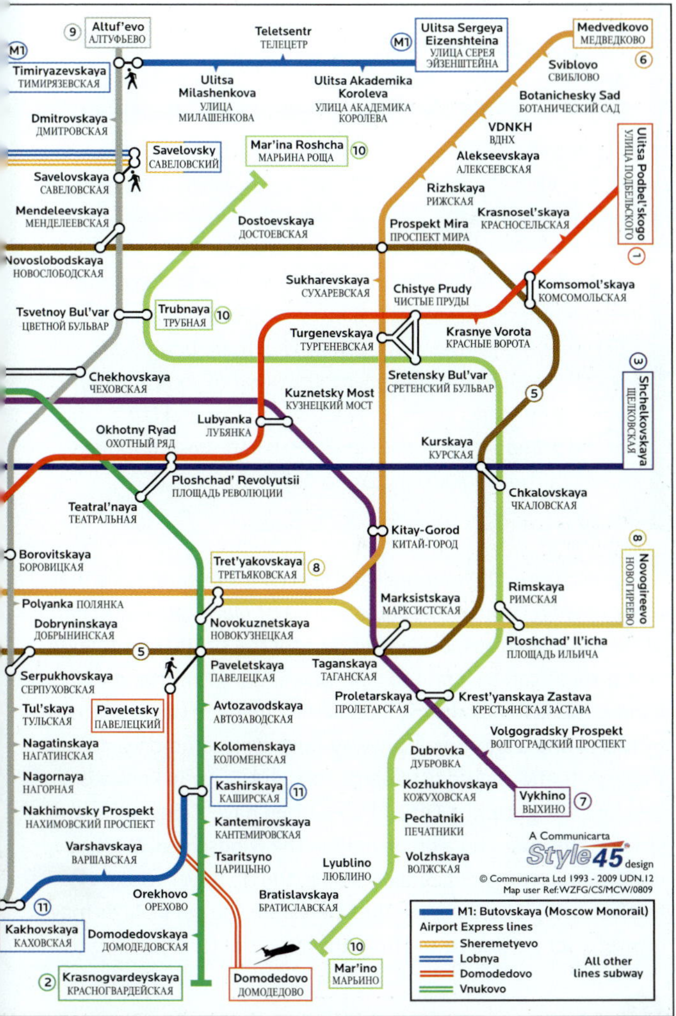

M1
Timiryazevskaya
ТИМИРЯЗЕВСКАЯ
9
Altuf'evo
АЛТУФЬЕВО
Teletsentr
ТЕЛЕЦЕТР
M1
Ulitsa Sergeya Eizenshteina
УЛИЦА СЕРЕЯ ЭЙЗЕНШТЕЙНА
Medvedkovo
МЕДВЕДКОВО
6
Ulitsa Milashenkova
УЛИЦА МИЛАШЕНКОВА
Ulitsa Akademika Koroleva
УЛИЦА АКАДЕМИКА КОРОЛЕВА
Sviblovo
СВИБЛОВО
Botanichesky Sad
БОТАНИЧЕСКИЙ САД
Dmitrovskaya
ДМИТРОВСКАЯ
VDNKH
ВДНХ
Savelovsky
САВЕЛОВСКИЙ
Mar'ina Roshcha
МАРЬИНА РОЩА
10
Alekseevskaya
АЛЕКСЕЕВСКАЯ
Ulitsa Podbel'skogo
УЛИЦА ПОДБЕЛЬСКОГО
Savelovskaya
САВЕЛОВСКАЯ
Rizhskaya
РИЖСКАЯ
Mendeleevskaya
МЕНДЕЛЕЕВСКАЯ
Dostoevskaya
ДОСТОЕВСКАЯ
Prospekt Mira
ПРОСПЕКТ МИРА
Krasnosel'skaya
КРАСНОСЕЛЬСКАЯ
1
Novoslobodskaya
НОВОСЛОБОДСКАЯ
Sukharevskaya
СУХАРЕВСКАЯ
Chistye Prudy
ЧИСТЫЕ ПРУДЫ
Komsomol'skaya
КОМСОМОЛЬСКАЯ
Tsvetnoy Bul'var
ЦВЕТНОЙ БУЛЬВАР
Trubnaya
ТРУБНАЯ
10
Turgenevskaya
ТУРГЕНЕВСКАЯ
Krasnye Vorota
КРАСНЫЕ ВОРОТА
3
Chekhovskaya
ЧЕХОВСКАЯ
Sretensky Bul'var
СРЕТЕНСКИЙ БУЛЬВАР
Shchelkovskaya
ЩЕЛКОВСКАЯ
Kuznetsky Most
КУЗНЕЦКИЙ МОСТ
5
Lubyanka
ЛУБЯНКА
Okhotny Ryad
ОХОТНЫЙ РЯД
Kurskaya
КУРСКАЯ
Ploshchad' Revolyutsii
ПЛОЩАДЬ РЕВОЛЮЦИИ
Chkalovskaya
ЧКАЛОВСКАЯ
Teatral'naya
ТЕАТРАЛЬНАЯ
Kitay-Gorod
КИТАЙ-ГОРОД
8
Borovitskaya
БОРОВИЦКАЯ
Tret'yakovskaya
ТРЕТЬЯКОВСКАЯ
8
Novogireevo
НОВОГИРЕЕВО
Rimskaya
РИМСКАЯ
Polyanka ПОЛЯНКА
Marksistskaya
МАРКСИСТСКАЯ
Dobryninskaya
ДОБРЫНИНСКАЯ
Novokuznetskaya
НОВОКУЗНЕЦКАЯ
Ploshchad' Il'icha
ПЛОЩАДЬ ИЛЬИЧА
5
Serpukhovskaya
СЕРПУХОВСКАЯ
Paveletskaya
ПАВЕЛЕЦКАЯ
Taganskaya
ТАГАНСКАЯ
Tul'skaya
ТУЛЬСКАЯ
Paveletsky
ПАВЕЛЕЦКИЙ
Avtozavodskaya
АВТОЗАВОДСКАЯ
Proletarskaya
ПРОЛЕТАРСКАЯ
Krest'yanskaya Zastava
КРЕСТЬЯНСКАЯ ЗАСТАВА
Nagatinskaya
НАГАТИНСКАЯ
Kolomenskaya
КОЛОМЕНСКАЯ
Volgogradsky Prospekt
ВОЛГОГРАДСКИЙ ПРОСПЕКТ
Dubrovka
ДУБРОВКА
Nagornaya
НАГОРНАЯ
Kashirskaya
КАШИРСКАЯ
11
Kozhukhovskaya
КОЖУХОВСКАЯ
Vykhino
ВЫХИНО
7
Nakhimovsky Prospekt
НАХИМОВСКИЙ ПРОСПЕКТ
Kantemirovskaya
КАНТЕМИРОВСКАЯ
Pechatniki
ПЕЧАТНИКИ
Varshavskaya
ВАРШАВСКАЯ
Tsaritsyno
ЦАРИЦЫНО
Lyublino
ЛЮБЛИНО
Volzhskaya
ВОЛЖСКАЯ
A Communicarta Style45 design
© Communicarta Ltd 1993 - 2009 UDN.12
Map user Ref:WZFG/CS/MCW/0809
Orekhovo
ОРЕХОВО
Bratislavskaya
БРАТИСЛАВСКАЯ
11
Kakhovskaya
КАХОВСКАЯ
Domodedovskaya
ДОМОДЕДОВСКАЯ
10
2
Krasnogvardeyskaya
КРАСНОГВАРДЕЙСКАЯ
Domodedovo
ДОМОДЕДОВО
Mar'ino
МАРЬИНО
M1: Butovskaya (Moscow Monorail)
Airport Express lines
Sheremetyevo
Lobnya
Domodedovo
Vnukovo
All other lines subway

THE MOSCOW METRO

Apart from being a subterranean work of art bedecked with ornate pieces of Socialist Realism, huge chandeliers and Soviet-era mosaics, the Moscow metro system is a very simple and user-friendly method of navigating your way around this colossal city. There are 12 colour-coded lines that generally run from one side of the city to the other and are all linked up by the brown circle line (*Koltsevaya*), which roughly follows the Garden Ring Road. Magnetic tickets, which are still remarkably cheap, are bought at booths beforehand, and once in the system you can chop and change lines as many times as you like, making a tour of the grandest stations a very cheap half-day out indeed. Services run from around 05.30 until around 01.00.

Buses, trams, the monorail and special fixed-route taxis that pick passengers up at bus stops and other places also form part of the Moscow transport system, but for the short-term foreign visitor these can be a bit too daunting and user-unfriendly to handle. The vast majority of places in the city centre can be reached by metro and a short walk anyway. Taxis are a common sight on the city's traffic-choked boulevards, though any car in Russia is a taxi for the right price. Official taxis often have a chequerboard strip on the door and a green light in the windscreen. Most taxi meters date from pre-Gorbachev days and no driver would ever think of using one, so agree the fare before you get in. Taxis may be useful for getting to and from the airport or for returning to

The monorail glides into Timiryazevskaya Station

your hotel late at night, but during Moscow's crazy rush-hour it's quicker to take the metro (or even walk!).

CAR HIRE

In a city the size of Moscow it may seem like a good idea to hire your own set of wheels to get around. Wrong! The sight of six lines of stationary traffic on a four-lane boulevard lost in a cloud of smog, or a luxury 4x4, lights blazing, haring down the middle of the road while Ladas and Volgas scuttle to the kerb to avoid head-on collisions will have you on the escalator down into the relative peace of the metro system in a flash. Moscow must be one of the worst places to drive in Europe, and most expats living in the city wouldn't dream of using a car to travel into the city centre. Things get even worse when you leave the city limits as there are the corrupt traffic police to deal with.

If, despite all the above, you still decide to rent, the following international agencies operate in the city. Some will not allow you to take the vehicle out of the city, others will supply the car with a driver! It goes without saying that rates are astronomical.

Avis ⓦ www.avis-moscow.ru

City centre: ⓐ Meschanskaya ul. 7/1 ⓣ (495) 744 0733 ◷ 09.00–18.00 Mon–Fri

Sheremetyevo 2 Airport: ⓣ (495) 578 7179 ◷ 06.00–00.00

Hertz ⓦ www.hertz.ru

City centre: ⓐ 1-st Brestskaya, 34 ⓣ (495) 232 0889 ◷ 09.00–21.00

Domodedovo Airport: ⓣ (495) 971 3056 ◷ 10.00–22.00

Sheremetyevo 2 Airport: ⓣ (495) 971 2065 ◷ 09.00–21.00

Towers and statues in Red Square

THE CITY OF
Moscow

Red Square, the Kremlin, Kitay-Gorod & Zamoskvareche

If the historical centre of Moscow were a Russian doll, then the Kremlin (see page 66) would be the tiniest figurine right at the core, with all the other districts like ever larger dolls slotting together around it. The very heart of the capital may be the smallest quarter in size, but it is without doubt the most historically significant, boasting many of Moscow's most instantly recognisable sights, such as Red Square (see page 65) and St Basil's Cathedral (see page 71) within its limits. If you are in Moscow for just a couple of days, this is where you will spend all of your time exploring the churches and cathedrals of the Kremlin, browsing the incredible collections of the State Tretyakov Gallery south of the River Moskva (see page 72) and gazing in awe at the cobbled expanse of Red Square. The Kitay-Gorod to the immediate northeast of Red Square is Moscow's historical commercial district. The name translates as 'China Town' but there is no evidence that any Chinese ever lived here: the name probably derived from *kita*, meaning wattle and referring to the wall which once protected the quarter. There's no ambiguity about the name Zamoskvareche, which literally means 'beyond the Moskva River'. The main draws here are the State Tretyakov Gallery and Gorky Park (see pages 72 & 65).

Red Square, the Kremlin and Kitay-Gorod can all be explored on foot. The main metro stations for Zamoskvareche are Tretyakovskaya and Oktyabrskaya. A novel way to tour at least a small part of the district is on board a boat on the Moskva River. The services

The Ivan the Great Bell Tower in the Kremlin

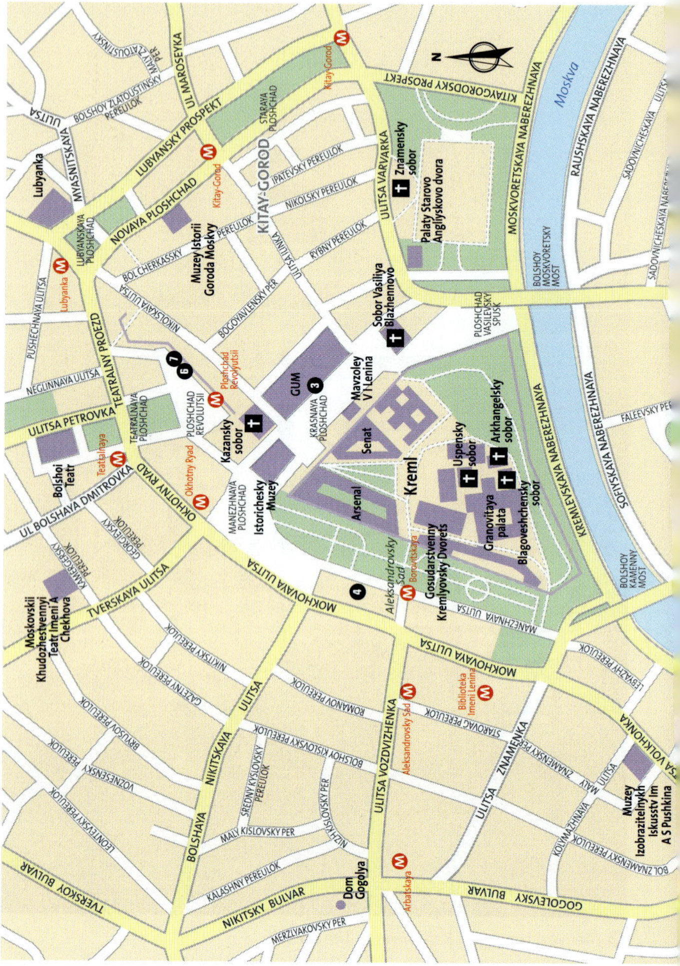
Lubyanka
Lubyanka
Lubyanskaya Ploshchad
Myasnitskaya Ulitsa
Bolshoy Zlatoustinsky Pereulok
Maly Zlatoustinsky Per
Ul Maroseyka
Lubyansky Prospekt
Novaya Ploshchad
Kitay-Gorod
Staraya Ploshchad
Muzey Istorii Goroda Moskvy
Kitay-Gorod
Ipatevsky Pereulok
Nikolsky Pereulok
Rybny Pereulok
Bol Cherkassky Pereulok
Ulitsa Ilyinka
Bogoyavlensky Per
Nikolskaya Ulitsa
Ulitsa Varvarka
Znamensky sobor
Palaty Starovo Angliyskovo dvora
Kitaygorodsky Prospekt
Moskvoretskaya Naberezhnaya
Moskva
Raushskaya Naberezhnaya
Sadovnicheskaya Ulitsa
Sadovnicheskaya Naberezhnaya
Bolshoy Moskvoretsky Most
Sobor Vasiliya Blazhennovo
Ploshchad Vasilevsky Spusk
Pushechnaya Ulitsa
Teatralny Proezd
Neglinnaya Ulitsa
Ulitsa Petrovka
Teatralnaya Ploshchad
Ploshchad Revolyutsii
Ploshchad Revolyutsii
GUM
Krasnaya Ploshchad
Mavzoley V I Lenina
Kazansky sobor
Senat
Kreml
Uspensky sobor
Arkhangelsky sobor
Kremlevskaya Naberezhnaya
Sofiyskaya Naberezhnaya
Faleevsky Per
Bolshoi Teatr
Teatralnaya
Okhotny Ryad
Okhotny Ryad
Istorichesky Muzey
Manezhnaya Ploshchad
Arsenal
Granovitaya palata
Blagoveshchensky sobor
Gosudarstvenny Kremlyovsky Dvorets
Aleksandrovsky Sad
Borovitskaya
Bolshoy Kamenny Most
Ul Bolshaya Dmitrovka
Georgievsky Pereulok
Kamergersky Pereulok
Tverskaya Ulitsa
Mokhovaya Ulitsa
Manezhnaya Ulitsa
Moskovskii Khudozhestvennyi Teatr Imeni A Chekhova
Nikitsky Pereulok
Gazetny Pereulok
Bryusov Pereulok
Voznesensky Pereulok
Leontevsky Pereulok
Romanov Pereulok
Biblioteka Imeni Lenina
Starovagankovsky Pereulok
Lebyazhy Pereulok
Volkhonka
Bolshaya Nikitskaya Ulitsa
Bolshoy Kislovsky Pereulok
Sredny Kislovsky Pereulok
Maly Kislovsky Per
Nizhny Kislovsky Per
Ulitsa Vozdvizhenka
Aleksandrovsky Sad
Ulitsa Znamenka
Znamensky Per
Maly Znamensky Per
Kolymazhnaya
Bol Znamensky Pereulok
Muzey Izobrazitelnykh Iskusstv Im A S Pushkina
Kalashny Pereulok
Tverskoy Bulvar
Nikitsky Bulvar
Merzlyakovsky Per
Dom Gogolya
Arbatskaya
Gogolevsky Bulvar

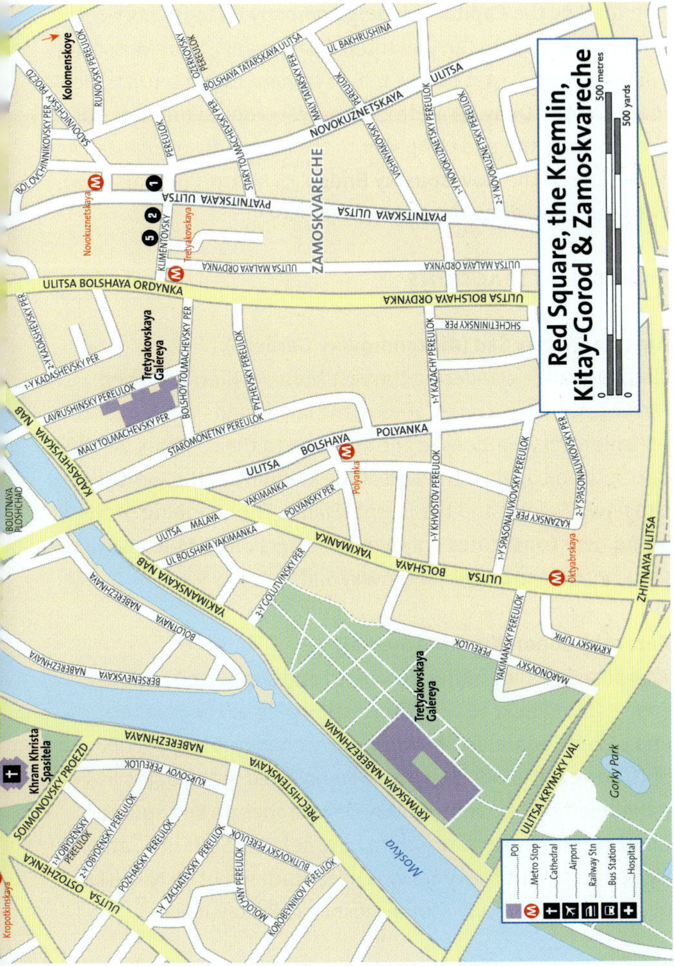
Red Square, the Kremlin, Kitay-Gorod & Zamoskvareche
0
500 metres
0
500 yards
POI
Metro Stop
Cathedral
Airport
Railway Stn
Bus Station
Hospital
Kolomenskoye
Novokuznetskaya
Tretyakovskaya
Polyanka
Oktyabrskaya
Kropotkinskaya
Tretyakovskaya Galereya
Tretyakovskaya Galereya
Khram Khrista Spasitela
ZAMOSKVARECHE
Gorky Park
Moskva
BOLOTNAYA PLOSHCHAD
ULITSA BOLSHAYA ORDYNKA
PYATNITSKAYA ULITSA
NOVOKUZNETSKAYA ULITSA
ULITSA MALAYA ORDYNKA
ULITSA BOLSHAYA POLYANKA
BOLSHAYA YAKIMANKA ULITSA
ULITSA MALAYA YAKIMANKA
UL BOLSHAYA YAKIMANKA
ZHITNAYA ULITSA
ULITSA KRYMSKY VAL
KRYMSKAYA NABEREZHNAYA
YAKIMANSKAYA NAB
KADASHEVSKAYA NAB
BOLOTNAYA NABEREZHNAYA
BERSENEVSKAYA NABEREZHNAYA
PRECHISTENSKAYA NABEREZHNAYA
SOIMONOVSKY PROEZD
ULITSA OSTOZHENKA
UL BAKHRUSHINA
BOLSHAYA TATARSKAYA ULITSA
KLIMENTOVSKY PEREULOK
LAVRUSHINSKY PEREULOK
MALY TOLMACHEVSKY PER
BOLSHOY TOLMACHEVSKY PER
STAROMONETNY PEREULOK
PYZHEVSKY PEREULOK
1-Y KAZACHY PEREULOK
1-Y KHVOSTOV PEREULOK
SHCHETININSKY PER
KAZANSKY PER
YAKIMANSKY PEREULOK
MAROONOVSKY PEREULOK
KRYMSKY TUPIK
KURSOVOY PEREULOK
BUTIKOVSKY PEREULOK
POZHARSKY PEREULOK
1-Y ZACHATEVSKY PEREULOK
MOLOCHNY PEREULOK
KOROBEYNIKOV PEREULOK
1-Y OBYDENSKY PEREULOK
2-Y OBYDENSKY PEREULOK
BOL OVCHINNIKOVSKY PER
SADOVNICHESKY PROEZD
RUNOVSKY PEREULOK
OZERKOVSKY PEREULOK
1-Y KADASHEVSKY PER
2-Y KADASHEVSKY PER
POLYANSKY PER
3-Y GOLUTVINSKY PER
1-Y SPASONALIVKOVSKY PEREULOK
2-Y SPASONALIVKOVSKY PER
VISHNYAKOVSKY PEREULOK
1-Y NOVOKUZNETSKY PEREULOK
2-Y NOVOKUZNETSKY PEREULOK
MALY TATARSKY PER
STARY TOLMACHEVSKY PER

operated by the **Capital Shipping Company** (t (495) 225 6070 w www.cck-ship.ru) carry all sorts of passengers, from Muscovites using the river to get from A to B to camera-toting tourists. Boats leave **Kievsky Quay** (Metro: Kievskaya) every 30 minutes during the day from the end of April until the beginning of October and terminate at the **Novospassky Bridge** (Metro: Proletarskaya), with six stops along the way.

SIGHTS & ATTRACTIONS

Aleksandrovsky Sad (Alexandrovsky Gardens)

Tired feet after wandering the vast Moscow Kremlin? Then recharge those batteries among the lawns and flower beds of Alexandrovsky Gardens at the entrance to the complex. At the northern end against the wall of the Kremlin lies the Tomb of the Unknown Soldier and the Eternal Flame. The changing of the guard here constitutes only a minor diversion. a Mokhovaya ul. 24 hrs Metro: Aleksandrovsky Sad

Kazansky Sobor (Kazan Cathedral)

This pleasing, diminutive, blood-red and snow-white church can be found next to the Resurrection gate at the northern end of Red Square. The building we see today is a 1993 copy of the original which Stalin had demolished in the 1930s as it hindered the progress of May Day parades on Red Square. Amazingly, a similar fate was to have befallen St Basil's Cathedral (see page 71), but the order was never carried out. a Nikolskaya ul. 3 08.00–18.00 Metro: Ploshchad Revolyutsii

GORKY PARK

At over 120 hectares (300 acres), this is by far the largest green space in the city centre and the best place to escape the noise and fumes of Moscow's roads to perhaps enjoy a picnic in peace. Within its leafy expanse next to the Moskva River you will discover a funfair with amusements and rides (including a retired Soviet space shuttle called the Buran), a sculpture park and one branch of the State Tretyakov Gallery (see page 72). In winter, the ponds freeze over, attracting skaters and there's even a skate hire booth on site. ⓐ Krymsky Val 7 ⓛ 10.00–21.00 Ⓝ Metro: Park Kultury

Krasnaya Ploshchad (Red Square)

Red Square is neither red nor square. The explanation behind its name is that Krasnaya Ploshchad (its Russian name) originally meant 'Beautiful Square', but in the 20th century the word *krasnaya* came to be synonymous with the colour red. If not exactly beautiful, Red Square is imposing, and its cobbled expanse immediately conjures up intimidating images of tanks, marching Red Army soldiers and long-range missiles you hoped you would never see hurtling towards your town, in the May Day parade during the Cold War decades. Today you are more likely to be obstructed on Moscow's most celebrated piazza by a crass Russian pop concert than a stern military parade, though most of the time it just swarms with bewildered tourists, postcard sellers and the odd pickpocket. Grouped around the square

are Moscow's premier sights, such as the Kremlin (see below), which fills the southwest flank, the Lenin Mausoleum (see page 67) northeast of the Kremlin, GUM (see page 74) along the northeastern side and St Basil's Cathedral (see page 71) guarding the south. Metro: Ploshchad Revolyutsii

Kreml (The Kremlin)

The Kremlin could be described as the star turn in Moscow's historical show and every visitor to the city should take at least half a day to visit its stately palaces and gleaming cathedrals. Many cities across Russia boast a *kremlin* (which simply means fort) but none come even close to Moscow's in grandeur and size.

Prince Yury Dolgoruky is believed to have erected the first wooden fortress on the site in the 12th century. Despite being attacked by the Mongols and then the Tatars, the Kremlin over the centuries steadily grew, in particular under the reigns of the two Ivans, Great and Terrible. Although Peter the Great moved the capital to St Petersburg in 1712, the Kremlin remained an important place where coronations, royal weddings and important religious ceremonies were held. Major rebuilding work took place after Napoleon's destructive sojourn in Moscow in 1812, and just over a century later Lenin moved the government back to Moscow to take up residence at the Kremlin. Communist bigwigs walked these corridors of power during the 70 years of Communist rule until 1991 when Boris Yeltsin moved in. The current Russian president resides in the Senate Palace.

Around two-thirds of the Kremlin's buildings are out of bounds to visitors, though that still leaves an incredible amount to see. Buy tickets and store bags at the ticket office in the Alexandrovsky

Gardens before entering through the Kutafya Tower. Cross the ramp and pass through the Trinity Tower, the highest in the Kremlin's walls. The Kremlin is roughly divided into two halves. On your left are the three huge buildings of the Arsenal, the Senate Palace and the Presidium. To your right stand the State Kremlin Palace, the Patriarch's Palace, the Great Kremlin Palace, the Armoury Palace and Diamond Fund Exhibition, the Terem Palace and Sobornaya ploshchad (Cathedral Square), around which are gathered the Archangel Cathedral, the Annunciation Cathedral, the Church of the Deposition of the Robe, the Cathedral of the Assumption, the Hall of Facets, the Ivan the Great Bell Tower and the Tsar Bell and Cannon.

Buying a Kremlin guidebook at the ticket office or hiring an expert English-speaking guide is a good idea if you want to know more. If you are short on time, the Armoury Palace full of imperial treasure, the golden-domed Cathedral of the Assumption and the Terem Palace are generally regarded as Kremlin highlights. ⓐ Aleksandrovsky Sad (ticket office) ⓣ (495) 965 4146 or (495) 695 3776 (info) ⓦ www.kremlin.museum.ru ◷ 10.00–18.00 Fri–Wed, mid-May–Sept; 10.00–17.00 Fri–Wed, Oct–mid-May (last entry half hour earlier) Ⓜ Metro: Aleksandrovsky Sad, Borovitskaya or Biblioteka Imeni Lenina. Admission charge

Mavzoley V I Lenina (Lenin Mausoleum)

The red granite and black marble functionalist tomb of 'Grandfather Lenin' can be found against the wall of the Kemlin facing the GUM department store (see page 74). Lenin's embalmed body has lain here since he died in 1924 (except for a brief evacuation to Siberia during World War II), and despite the revolutionary's own personal wish to be buried next to his mother in St Petersburg and the end of Communist rule in 1991, the waxy body remains one of the most popular tourist attractions in the capital (possibly as it's free to get in). A team of scientists treat the corpse with a secret mixture of chemicals every day and, every 18 months, Lenin is removed for a complete service. A visit to the tomb is a sombre affair with cheerless guards making sure foreigners in particular act in a suitably respectful manner (no hands in pockets). There's no time to linger at the body itself and a minute after paying your respects to one of Russia's best known 20th-century figures you'll emerge blinking into the light of sunny/snowy Red Square. ⓐ Red Square ⓣ (495) 623 5527 ⓛ 10.00–13.00 Tues–Thur, Sat & Sun ⓜ Metro: Ploshchad Revolyutsii ⓘ All cameras and bags must be stored at the State Historical Museum (see page 71) before entering the mausoleum

Palaty Starovo Angliyskovo dvora (Old English Court)

Varvarka Street, which connects the southern end of Red Square with the Inner Ring Road, is one of Moscow's most attractive thoroughfares, lined as it is with pretty domed churches (the most in any one street in the city) and historical buildings. Perhaps the most interesting feature is the English Court, a reconstructed 16th-century house which once served as a residence for English emissaries during the reign of Ivan the Terrible and opened as a museum to coincide with a state visit by Queen Elizabeth II in 1994. ⓐ ul. Varvarka 4a ⓣ (495) 698 3952 ⓦ www.mosmuseum.ru ⓛ 10.00–18.00 Mon–Fri ⓜ Metro: Kitay-Gorod. Admission charge

Colourful St Basil's Cathedral peppered with snow

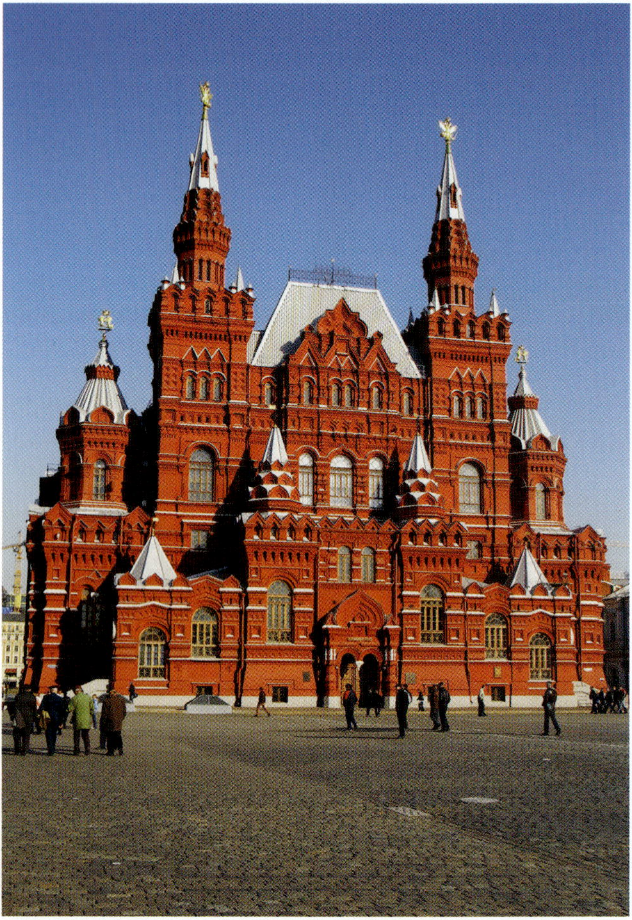

The State Historical Museum sits on the northern edge of Red Square

Sobor Vasiliya Blazhennovo (St Basil's Cathedral)

The riot of a cathedral at the southern end of Red Square is one of the Russian capital's most instantly recognisable sights and surely its most photographed building. While most people's idea of an orthodox church is based on St Basil's, the cathedral is quite a unique example and rather untypical. However, this was not always the case as it only received its *Technicolor* makeover in 1670. Even the original building was an ornate affair and it is said Ivan the Terrible, having commissioned the church to celebrate the capture of Kazan, had the builders' eyes put out when they completed it in 1561, lest they repeat the feat in another city (standard practice among medieval tyrants). The psychedelic décor of the cupolas continues on the inside with various chapels decorated in multicoloured patterns. ⓐ Krasnaya pl. ⓣ (495) 698 3304 ⓒ 11.00–17.30 ⓜ Metro: Ploshchad Revolyutsii. Admission charge

CULTURE

Gosudarstvenny Kremlyovsky Dvorets (State Kremlin Palace)

Most make a beeline for the Bolshoi Theatre to see ballet (see page 85), but the classical repertoire at the Kremlin is just as good, even though the venue is not quite as grand. ⓐ Vozdvizhenka 1 ⓣ (495) 628 5232 or (495) 917 2336 (info) ⓦ www.gkd.ru ⓜ Metro: Aleksandrovsky Sad

Istorichesky Muzey (State Historical Museum)

Dominating the northern end of Red Square, the State Historical Museum should be high on the list of sights for anyone with even a passing interest in Russian history. Housed in a brick-red late 19th-century building sporting all manner of turrets and saw-tooth gables, exhibits stretch from pre-history to the 19th century and cover the entire Russian Empire (half the globe, basically). The richly decorated interior alone is worth the admission charge, and it's a great option for a rainy day as there's enough to keep you occupied for hours. ⓐ Krasnaya pl. 1 ⓣ (495) 692 4019 ⓦ www.shm.ru ⓛ 10.00–18.00 Mon, Wed–Sat, 11.00–19.00 Sun (ticket office closes 1 hr earlier) ⓜ Metro: Ploshchad Revolyutsii. Admission charge

Muzey Istorii Goroda Moskvy (Moscow History Museum)
Housed in a former church, this small museum traces the growth of Moscow from wooden fort to megalopolis with particular focus on the city in medieval times. ⓐ Novaya pl. 12 ⓣ (495) 624 8490 ⓦ www.mosmuseum.ru ⓛ 10.00–18.00 Tues, Thur, Sat & Sun, 11.00–19.00 Wed, Fri (last entry half hour earlier) ⓜ Metro: Lubyanka ⓘ Closed last Fri of month. Admission charge

Tretyakovskaya Galereya (State Tretyakov Gallery)
Apart from Gorky Park (see page 65), the main reason for travelling south of the river is to visit one of the best art museums in Russia, the State Tretyakov Gallery, which possesses the world's premier collection of Russian art exhibited at two sites. The Old Tretyakov starts with medieval icons and frescoes and ends at the 19th century. Some of the best known works on display are by 14th-century monk, Andrei Rublyev, the most famous Russian icon painter. The New Tretyakov in Gorky Park takes up where the Old Tretyakov leaves off with a fascinating

State Tretyakov Gallery houses the world's best Russian art

exhibition of 20th-century art, including many examples of Socialist Realism.

Old Tretyakov Gallery ⓐ Lavrushinsky per. 10 ⓣ (499) 238 1378 ⓦ www.tretyakovgallery.ru ⓛ 10.00–19.30 Tues–Sun (last entry 19.00) ⓜ Metro: Tretyakovskaya. Admission charge

New Tretyakov Gallery ⓐ ul. Krymsky Val 10 ⓣ (499) 230 7788 ⓦ www.tretyakovgallery.ru ⓛ 10.00–19.30 Tues–Sun (last entry 19.00) ⓜ Metro: Oktyabrskaya. Admission charge

RETAIL THERAPY

GUM Those who were lucky enough to visit the USSR in the 1970s and 80s will remember GUM (which stands for Gosudarstvenny Univermag or State Department Store) for its endless queues and empty shelves. Come and see how times have changed at what is now one of Moscow's glossiest high-end department stores, and definitely the most famous in all of Russia. ⓐ Red Square 3 ⓣ (495) 788 4343 ⓦ www.gum.ru ⓛ 10.00–22.00 ⓜ Metro: Ploshchad Revolyutsii

Okhotny Ryad Shopping Centre No expense was spared when Moscow mayor, Yury Luzhkov, was creating this subterranean retail experience on Manezhnaya ploshchad. Though decorated in imitation marble and gold leaf, the mall is not particularly exclusive and contains all kinds of outlets attracting the widest possible spectrum of shoppers. There's a food court on the lower level as well as a cinema. ⓐ Manezhnaya pl. 1/2 ⓣ (495) 737 8449 ⓦ www.oxotniy.ru ⓛ 10.00–22.00 ⓜ Metro: Okhotny Ryad

TAKING A BREAK

Grably £–££ ❶ An excellent value self-service restaurant, situated over three levels of a 19th-century art nouveau building. ⓐ ul. Pyatnitskaya 27 ⓣ (495) 545 0831 ⓦ www.grably.ru ⓛ 09.00–23.00 ⓜ Metro: Novokuznetskaya

Apshu ££ ❷ By day this is a simple, laid-back café serving a tasty selection of salads, *zakuski* (snacks), soups, pasta, fish and meat dishes in modest surroundings, but every evening it is transformed into a folk and jazz venue which sees the vodka and cocktails flow till the early hours. ⓐ Klimentovsky per. 10/1 ⓣ (495) 953 9944 ⓦ www.apshu.ru ⓛ 24 hrs ⓜ Metro: Tretyakovskaya

Bosco £££ ❸ A convenient but expensive café in the GUM shopping centre serving a mix of Italian, Russian and international dishes. Most people come here to sip a cappuccino and enjoy the views of Red Square and St Basil's Cathedral. ⓐ Red Square 3 (GUM) ⓣ (495) 627 3703 ⓦ www.bosco.ru ⓜ Metro: Ploshchad Revolyutsii

AFTER DARK

Albion £–££ ❹ If you're feeling homesick, head to this slice of England in the Manezh shopping centre. Here you can drink a pint of English ale or cider and enjoy a Russian version of fish and chips. ⓐ Manezhnaya pl. 1/2 (upper level) ⓣ (495) 995 9554 ⓦ www.albion-pub.ru ⓛ 12.00–00.00 ⓜ Metro: Okhotny Ryad

The Yellow Hall is just one of the decorative dining rooms at Godunov

Matryoshka ££ ❺ Close to the State Tretyakov Gallery, this restaurant serves both Russian and Ukrainian cuisine. The house speciality is *borsch* in a ceramic pot sealed with bread and *vareniki* (potato dumplings). ⓐ Klimentovsky per. 10/2 ⓣ (495) 953 9400 ⓛ 11.00–00.00 ⓜ Metro: Tretyakovskaya

Godunov £££ ❻ Housed in the former Zaikonospassky Monastery, this is one of the most richly ornate and opulent restaurants you will ever visit. The three dining spaces boast intricately painted ceilings which curve right down to the floor, tables are beautifully laid and service swift. Definitely not for those on any sort of budget. ⓐ Teatralnaya pl. 5 ⓣ (495) 698 4490 ⓦ www.godunov.net ⓛ 12.00–00.00 ⓜ Metro: Teatralnaya/Ploschad Revolyutsii ⓘ Booking essential

Staraya Bashnya £££ ❼ The 'Old Tower' is another very central eatery just a few steps northeast of Red Square. It's known for its exquisitely prepared Russian cuisine, serving dishes such as duck with apple and reindeer steaks in wild berry sauce. There's live music most nights, usually a Russian folk ensemble. ⓐ Teatralnaya pl. 5/1 ⓣ (495) 698 4008 ⓛ 12.00–00.00 ⓜ Metro: Ploshchad Revolyutsii

Beliy Gorod

With more time to explore the Russian capital, the Beliy Gorod (White Town), a horseshoe-shaped strip of cityscape wedged between the Inner Ring Road and the Boulevard Ring Road, is the next obvious destination after the Kremlin and Red Square. While Moscow's inner core possesses most of the city's historical heritage, the Beliy Gorod enjoys some of its more highbrow diversions such as the Bolshoi Theatre (see page 85) and the Pushkin Museum of Fine Arts (see page 85). The quarter also has some exciting shopping possibilities, with yet more chic malls and two of Moscow's better outlet-lined streets – Tverskaya and Petrovka. The Beliy Gorod provides an insight into the dark side of the Soviet decades in the shape of the much feared Lubyanka Building, the former KGB headquarters (see page 82). The building still houses the Russian security service, albeit rebranded as 'FSB'. The quarter's latest addition is the huge Cathedral of Christ the Saviour (see below), whose massive white spires and gilt domes dominate the embankment of the Moskva River.

Getting around the White Town is just about manageable on foot, though there are ample metro stations on hand. Purple line 7 and red line 1 are particularly useful here.

SIGHTS & ATTRACTIONS

Khram Khrista Spasitela (Cathedral of Christ the Saviour)

Visitors to Moscow carrying old maps will be surprised to find a huge, ancient-looking gold-domed church where there should be a large, outdoor swimming pool! This mammoth cathedral is

Cathedral of Christ the Saviour

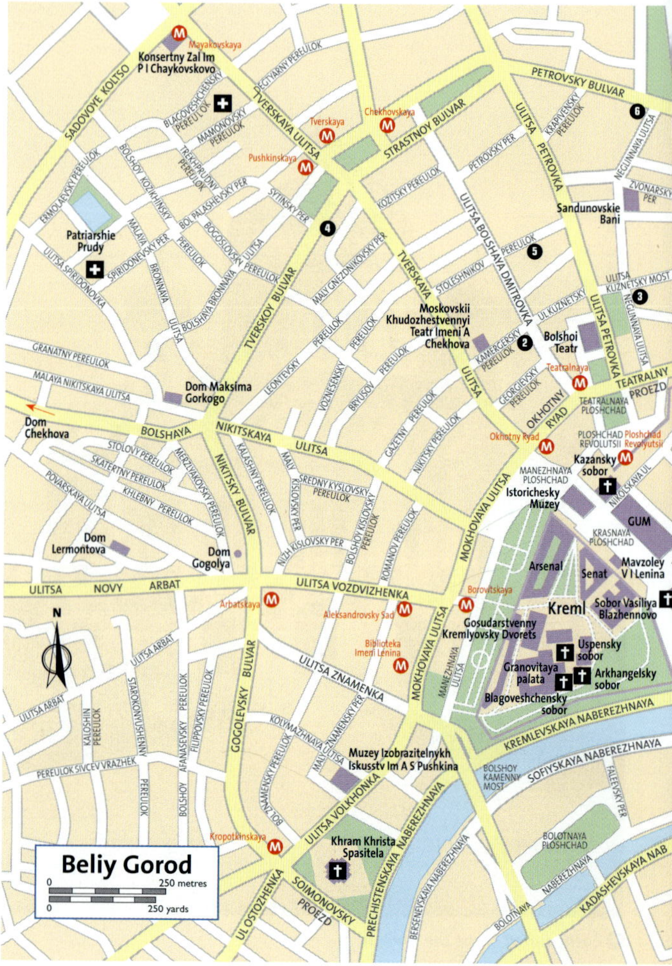
Beliy Gorod
0 250 metres
0 250 yards
Konsertny Zal Im P I Chaykovskovo
Mayakovskaya
Tverskaya
Chekhovskaya
Pushkinskaya
Patriarshie Prudy
Sandunovskie Bani
Moskovskii Khudozhestvennyi Teatr Imeni A Chekhova
Bolshoi Teatr
Teatralnaya
Dom Maksima Gorkogo
Dom Chekhova
Okhotny Ryad
Ploshchad Revolyutsii
Kazansky sobor
Istorichesky Muzey
GUM
Dom Lermontova
Dom Gogolya
Arsenal
Senat
Mavzoley V I Lenina
Kreml
Sobor Vasiliya Blazhennovo
Borovitskaya
Arbatskaya
Aleksandrovsky Sad
Gosudarstvenny Kremlyovsky Dvorets
Biblioteka Imeni Lenina
Uspensky sobor
Granovitaya palata
Arkhangelsky sobor
Blagoveshchensky sobor
Muzey Izobrazitelnykh Iskusstv Im A S Pushkina
Kropotkinskaya
Khram Khrista Spasitela
SADOVOYE KOLTSO
TVERSKAYA ULITSA
STRASTNOY BULVAR
PETROVSKY BULVAR
ULITSA PETROVKA
TVERSKOY BULVAR
ULITSA BOLSHAYA DMITROVKA
BOLSHAYA NIKITSKAYA ULITSA
NIKITSKY BULVAR
MOKHOVAYA ULITSA
TEATRALNY PROEZD
OKHOTNY RYAD
ULITSA NOVY ARBAT
ULITSA VOZDVIZHENKA
ULITSA ZNAMENKA
GOGOLEVSKY BULVAR
ULITSA ARBAT
KREMLEVSKAYA NABEREZHNAYA
SOFIYSKAYA NABEREZHNAYA
PRECHISTENSKAYA NABEREZHNAYA
ULITSA VOLKHONKA
SOIMONOVSKY PROEZD
UL OSTOZHENKA
KADASHEVSKAYA NAB
BOLOTNAYA PLOSHCHAD
BOLSHOY KAMENNY MOST
MANEZHNAYA PLOSHCHAD
TEATRALNAYA PLOSHCHAD
KRASNAYA PLOSHCHAD
PLOSHCHAD REVOLUTSII
N

Red Gates Administrative Building
Krasnye Vorota
BOL SERGIEVSKY PEREULOK
KOLOKOLNIKOV PEREULOK
PECHATNIKOV PEREULOK
UL STRETENKA
LUKOV PEREULOK
KOSTYANSKY PEREULOK
PROSPEKT AKADEMIKA SAKHAROVA
MYASNITSKAYA ULITSA
MALY KHARITONOVSKY PER
BOL KOZLOVSKY PEREULOK
SADOVOYE KOLTSO
BASMANNY TUPIK
ROZHDESTVENSKY BULVAR
SRETENSKY BULVAR
PLOSHCHAD MYASNITSKIE VOROTA
Turgenevskaya
Chistye Prudy
PER OGORODNOY SLOBODY
BOLSHOY KHARITONEVSKY PEREULOK
FURMANNY PEREULOK
ULITSA MASHKOVA
BOL KISELNY PEREULOK
MILYUTINSKY PEREULOK
ULITSA MALAYA LUBYANKA
ULITSA BOLSHAYA LUBYANKA
CHISTOPRUDNY BULVAR
ULITSA ZHUKOVSKOGO
ULITSA CHAPLYGINA
Kuznetsky Most
MYASNITSKAYA ULITSA
KRIVOKOLENNY PEREULOK
ARKHANGELSKY PEREULOK
POTAPOVSKY PEREULOK
ARMYANSKY PEREULOK
SVERCHKOV PEREULOK
ULITSA POKROVKA
Lubyanka
LUBYANSKAYA PLOSHCHAD
BOL ZLATOUSTINSKY PEREULOK
MAL ZLATOUSTINSKY PEREULOK
BARASHEVSKIY PEREULOK
BOL KAZENNY PEREULOK
LYALIN PEREULOK
NOVAYA PLOSHCHAD
LUBYANSKY PROSPEKT
ULITSA MAROSEYKA
ULITSA POKROVKA
STAROSADSKY PEREULOK
PODSOSENSKY PEREULOK
POKROVSKY BULVAR
PLOSHCHAD KURSKOGO VOKZALA
Muzey Istorii Goroda Moskvy
Kitay-Gorod
BOL SPASOGLINISHCHEVSKY PER
PETROVERIGSKY PEREULOK
KOLPACHNY PER
KHOKHLOVSKY PER
Chkalovskaya
ULITSA ILINKA
NIKOLSKY PEREULOK
IPATEVSKY PEREULOK
STARAYA PLOSHCHAD
RYBNY PEREULOK
UL ZABELINA
BOL TREKHSVYATITELSKY PEREULOK
MALY TREKHSVYATITELSKY PEREULOK
DURASOVSKY PER
ULITSA VORONTSOVO POLE
ULITSA ZEMLYANOY VAL
Kitay-Gorod
SOLYANSKY TUPIK
ULITSA VARVARKA
Znamensky sobor
Palaty Starovo Angliyskovo dvora
KITAYGORODSKY PROSPEKT
ULITSA SOLYANKA
PODKOLOKOLNY PER
YAUZSKY BULVAR
BOL NIKOLOVOROBINSKY PEREULOK
PEREULOK OBUKHA
Muzey Sakharova
VOSPITATELNY PROEZD
PLOSHCHAD YAUZSKIE VOROTA
SEREBRYANICHESKY PEREULOK
SEREBRYANICHESKAYA NABEREZHNAYA
BERNIKOVSKAYA NABEREZHNAYA
MOSKVORETSKAYA NABEREZHNAYA
Moskva
USTINSKY PROEZD
YAUZSKAYA ULITSA
RAUSHSKAYA NABEREZHNAYA
NIKOLOYAMSKAYA ULITSA
BOLSHOY VATIN PEREULOK
SADOVNICHESKAYA ULITSA
SADOVNICHESKAYA NABEREZHNAYA
BOLSHOY USTINSKY MOST
KOTELNICHESKAYA NABEREZHNAYA
Kotelnicheskaya Embankment Building
OVCHINNIKOVSKAYA NAB
KOSMODAMIANSKAYA NAB
TETERINSKY PEREULOK
BOLDROVYANOY PEREULOK
SRED OVCHINNIKOVSKY PEREULOK
GONCHARNAYA ULITSA
SADOVNICHESKY PROEZD
PYATNITSKAYA ULITSA
Taganskaya
TAGANSKAYA PLOSHCHAD
Novokuznetskaya
POI
Metro Stop
Cathedral
Airport
Railway Stn
Bus Station
Hospital

a late 1990s, $360 million copy of the building which stood on the site until 1933, when Stalin had it dynamited to make way for the Palace of the Soviets, a mammoth project which was to have been crowned with a giant statue of Lenin (some claim his extended index finger would have contained an entire cinema). This was never built and an open-air swimming pool was created instead. The cathedral interior is a grandly decorated affair, with every surface covered in religious paintings and gold leaf. The no-expense-spared feel gives some indication of the current power and wealth of the Russian Orthodox Church. After looking reverently around the cathedral, visit the small museum (also free) beneath the building. ⓐ ul. Volkhonka 15 ⓣ (495) 637 2847 ⓦ www.xxc.ru
🕒 13.00–17.00 Mon, 10.00–17.00 Tues–Sun Ⓜ Metro: Kropotkinskaya

Lubyanka (Lubyanka Building)

This granite-and-red-sandstone edifice on Lubyanskaya ploshchad was once the most feared building in all Russia. The headquarters of the USSR's infamous security service, the KGB, was built on the site of a secret prison used during the reign of Catherine the Great. During Stalin's repressions, this was terror central, with thousands executed in its underground prison. A popular Communist-era joke went that the Lubyanka enjoyed a great view: from there you could see Siberia! Until 1991, a statue of Dzerzhinsky, who founded the security service (the Cheka) during the 1917 revolution, stood in the middle of the square. The Lubyanka is still the headquarters of a resurgent Russian security service (and therefore not open to visitors), which underwent a kind of rebranding exercise after the fall of Communism, and now calls itself the FSB.
ⓐ Lubyanskaya pl. Ⓜ Metro: Lubyanka

Lubyanka is the HQ of the Russian security service

Sandunovskie Bani (Sandunovsky Baths)

Some say that if you haven't experienced the Russian *banya* or baths (see below), you haven't experienced Russia – well, that's maybe a slight exaggeration, but the *banya*, a kind of Russian take on the sauna, is a tradition you shouldn't miss, if only to scrub the city out of your hair. The Sandunovsky Baths are the oldest

THE BATHHOUSE

From Moscow's Sandunovsky Baths to a timber shack in the Siberian *taiga*, the *banya* is an integral part of life across the Russian Federation. Russians believe that steaming rids the body of toxins, stress and various aches and pains, and brings the soul back to life. Slightly more the preserve of men than women, it is also an occasion for chatting, drinking tea and socialising.

There are three parts to every *banya*: a changing room, a washing room and the steam room itself. In larger *banyas* there may also be a cold-water pool and a sauna. Undress in the changing room, wrap yourself in the sheet provided and prepare to be steamed alive. Water is ladled onto the hot rocks and the cleansing process begins. After several minutes of this, dive into the cold pool for an amazing sensation all over the body. This is repeated several times with the option of being whipped by fellow bathers with birch twigs if you are so inclined. The final step is to take a shower, after which you will leave feeling cleansed, tingling and refreshed.

and most famous in Moscow, and were once frequented by Chekhov and Tolstoy. Now anyone can steam, scrub, lather and whip their body until raw in elegant 19th-century surroundings. ⓐ Neglinnaya ul. 14/3–7 ⓣ (495) 625 4631 ⓦ www.sanduny.ru ⓛ 08.00–22.00 Ⓜ Metro: Kuznetsky Most or Trubnaya. Admission charge

CULTURE

Bolshoi Teatr (Bolshoi Theatre)

A quintessentially Russian experience and essential viewing if you can get tickets, a night at the world's most famous ballet will be the romantic highlight of any break in Moscow (and it won't cost you a fortune like it does back home). The theatre hosts ballet and opera in equal measure, though it's the performances of Tchaikovsky's *Nutcracker* and *Swan Lake* that everyone longs to see. The historical stage of the Bolshoi is under reconstruction until 2011; in the meantime performances take place on a modern stage just next to the main building. ⓐ Teatralnaya pl. 1 ⓣ (495) 250 7317 ⓦ www.bolshoi.ru Ⓜ Metro: Teatralnaya ⓘ Book tickets well in advance

Muzey Izobrazitelnykh Iskusstv Im. A S Pushkina (Pushkin Museum of Fine Arts)

Moscow's answer to the St Petersburg Hermitage holds huge collections of art from Byzantine and Greek to Post-Impressionist and Cubist. There are works by Van Gogh, Matisse, Picasso, Chagall, Toulouse-Lautrec, Monet, Rembrandt, Canaletto, Rubens, El Greco, Botticelli, Tintoretto and many other heavyweights of art history. Due to the vast amount of works the museum holds in its stores, exhibits are rotated, so what you see this time may not be hanging there the next. Allow at least half a day to see all the rooms. ⓐ ul. Volkhonka 12 ⓣ (495) 609 9520 ⓦ www.museum.ru/gmii ⓛ 10.00–19.00 Tues, Wed, Fri–Sun, 10.00–21.00 Thur ⓜ Metro: Kropotkinskaya. Admission charge

RETAIL THERAPY

Petrovsky Passazh (Petrovsky Passage) Another glitzy shopping centre where shopaholics can get their fix of retail mania. This is one of the more luxurious places to flash the plastic, with pricey designer-label stores catering for the daily needs of Moscow's oil-flushed nouveau riche. The building, with its arching glass roof, is worth a look even if you can't afford to buy anything. ⓐ ul. Petrovka 10 ⓣ (495) 692 9005 ⓛ 10.00–22.00 Mon–Sat, 10.00–20.00 Sun ⓜ Metro: Kuznetsky Most

TsUM Most cities across the former USSR have (or had) a TsUM, but Moscow's Central Department Store (Tsentralny Universalny Magazin) has most certainly shaken off its proletariat image and is now a temple to expensive brand names and designer labels. ⓐ ul. Petrovka 2 ⓣ (495) 933 7300 ⓦ www.tsum.ru ⓛ 10.00–22.00 Mon–Sat, 11.00–22.00 Sun ⓜ Metro: Teatralnaya

Yeliseevsky Gastronom (Yeliseev's Food Hall) Known as Gastronom No. 1 in Soviet times, this exquisite deli was well stocked even then. With its chandeliers, carved mahogany shelves, large glass display cabinets and tiled floors, it may slightly remind visitors of the food court at Harrods and is

The opulent interior of Yeliseev's Food Hall

the most lavish emporium to visit for vodka, champagne, caviar, chocolates and many other Russian goodies. ⓐ Tverskaya ul. 14 ⓣ (495) 650 0760 ⓦ www.eliseevskiy.ru ⓛ 24 hrs ⓜ Metro: Pushkinskaya, Tverskaya or Chekhovskaya

TAKING A BREAK

Coffee Bean £ ❶ This is the original branch of a Western-style chain of coffee shops that has spread across the city. The lattes and cappuccinos are on the pricey side but provide a decent enough caffeine fix and the interior is attractive. The ideal place for a coffee stop after a spot of shopping. ⓐ ul. Pokrovka 18/3 ⓣ (495) 623 9793 ⓦ www.coffebean.ru ⓛ 08.00–23.00 ⓜ Metro: Chistye Prudy or Kitay-Gorod

Seno £–££ ❷ The ideal option if you can't afford Moscow's restaurants, with a cheap, eat-as-much-as-you-like buffet laden with belly-filling Russian and international favourites. Popular among students and foreign tourists, possibly thanks to the very reasonably priced ales on tap. ⓐ Kamergersky per. 6 ⓣ (495) 692 0452 ⓛ 10.00–23.00 ⓜ Metro: Teatralnaya or Okhotny Ryad

Yolki Palki ££ ❸ A very popular local chain of restaurants with a kitschy rustic theme. The Russian food is inexpensive, hearty and comes in farmers' portions. Many migrate here in the evening for a cheap bevvy out on the terrace. ⓐ Neglinnaya ul. 8/10 ⓣ (495) 628 5525 ⓦ www.elki-palki.ru ⓜ 10.00–00.00 Mon–Fri, 11.00–00.00 Sat & Sun ⓜ Metro: Kuznetsky Most

AFTER DARK

RESTAURANTS

Café Pushkin £££ ❹ Many a Muscovite will be impressed to hear you've dined at Café Pushkin, often referred to as the best restaurant in Russia. However, such a boast will not come cheap. This 19th-century classic has a less expensive ground-floor café and a more exclusive upper floor, where a main dish can cost over 1,200 roubles. Service is impeccable, the food could not be better and the whole experience is extremely civilised. ⓐ Tverskoy bul. 26a ⓣ (495) 739 0033 ⓦ www.cafe-pushkin.ru ⓛ Café: 24 hrs; restaurant: 12.00–23.30 ⓜ Metro: Pushkinskaya

Guilly's Steak & Seafood House (Gilyay) £££ ❺ Slightly off the beaten tourist track, Guilly's is an affordable steakhouse popular with expats. A calm, relaxing atmosphere, excellent service and big juicy steaks are the order of the day here. ⓐ Stoleshnikov per. 6 ⓣ (495) 933 5521 ⓛ 12.00–00.00 ⓜ Metro: Teatralnaya, Pushkinskaya or Chekhovskaya

Uzbekistan £££ ❻ This is a classic, long-established, Central Asian restaurant and one of the best options in town if you are looking for an alternative to Russian fare. Traditional Uzbek dishes you should try are *plov* (spicy rice with diced meat and carrots), *shurpa* (meat broth), *ugra* (noodle soup), *chuchvara* (mutton or beef ravioli), *manty* (golf-ball-sized steamed dumplings filled with meat, eaten across Central Asia and Eastern Siberia) and *lagman* (spaghetti in vegetable sauce). The menu also features superb Middle Eastern and Chinese fare. Portion sizes here are

Try the great menu in the lush interior of Uzbekistan

generous and half portions come for half the price. Combine all this with live music and nightly belly dancing and you have an exotic night out, Tashkent-style. ⓐ Neglinnaya ul. 29/14 ⓣ (495) 628 5525 ⓦ www.uzbek-rest.ru ⓛ 12.00–late ⓜ Metro: Trubnaya

CLUBS

Bilingua Arty club, cheap café, book/CD store and hippy clothes shop rolled into one with live music every night of the week, very cheap beer and a quite un-Russian vibe. Some complain of slow service and too much smoke, not all of it emanating from conventional cigarettes. ⓐ Krivokolenny per. 10/5 ⓣ (495) 623 9660 ⓦ www.bilinguaclub.ru ⓛ 24 hrs ⓜ Metro: Turgenevskaya or Lubyanka

Propaganda Café by day, club by night, this laid-back, gay-friendly place is popular among locals, expats and tourists. You can have a steak here for lunch then come back in the evening to dance it off. Highly recommended. ⓐ Bolshoi Zlatoustinsky per. 7 ⓣ (495) 924 5732 ⓦ www.propagandamoscow.com ⓛ 11.30–06.00 ⓜ Metro: Kitay-Gorod

Solyanka Considered one of the trendiest clubs in Moscow, this is an excellent place to dance the night away in safety. ⓐ ul. Solyanka 11 ⓣ (495) 221 7557 ⓦ http://s-11.ru/klub ⓛ 10.00–00.00 Mon–Wed, 23.00–06.00 Thu–Sat ⓜ Metro: Kitay-Gorog

Zemlyanoy Gorod

The Zemlyanoy Gorod or 'Earth Town' forms the next half-circle out from the Beliy Gorod between the Boulevard Ring Road and the Garden Ring Road. It extends in a sweeping arch from the Moskva River in the southwest to Moscow's second river, the Yauza, to the east of the city centre. This huge swathe of Moscow gets its name from the earthen rampart which ran around its circumference in medieval times. It is defined by the Garden Ring Road, once a leafy, tree-lined thoroughfare, but transformed into a thundering eight-lane highway in the 1930s. Underground, the brown circle metro line roughly follows the Garden Ring Road, or you can also hop aboard trolleybus B, which provides a very cheap hour-long tour (traffic permitting) of the entire ring.

Here you'll find Moscow's most touristy street, the Arbat, a bohemian thoroughfare famous for its street life, souvenir stalls and café culture. On the cultural front, the houses of celebrated literary figures including Gogol, Tolstoy and Chekhov have been turned into museums dedicated to their work (see page 100). Although not strictly located in Zemlyanoy Gorod, the excellent Kolomenskoye complex in the southeast of the city is easily reached by metro from here and warrants at least a half-day visit.

SIGHTS & ATTRACTIONS

The Arbat

Ulitsa Novy Arbat and the surrounding lanes, once Moscow's bohemian quarter, have gone the way of most European urban arty districts with the tourists, trinket sellers and money-makers

Moscow University – with the tallest tower of the Seven Sisters skyscrapers

POI
Metro Stop
Cathedral
Airport
Railway Stn
Bus Station
Hospital
Belorussky vokzal
Belorusskaya
Novoslobodskaya
NIZHNYAYA ULITSA
PLOSHCHAD TVERSKOY ZASTAVY
LESNAYA ULITSA
MIUSSKAYA PLOSHCHAD
KRASNOPROLETARSKAYA ULITSA
DOLGORUKOVSKAYA ULITSA
1-Y SAMOTECHNY PEREULOK
DELEGATSKAYA ULITSA
UL GRUZINSKY VAL
1-YA TVERSKAYA-YAMSKAYA ULITSA
2-YA BRESTSKAYA ULITSA
1-YA BRESTSKAYA ULITSA
ULITSA CHAYANOVA
ULITSA FADEEVA
ORUZHEYNY PEREULOK
SADOVOYE KOLTSO
Novaya Opera
MALAYA DMITROVKA ULITSA
UL KARETNY RYAD
LIKHOV PEREULOK
Tsvetnoy Bulvar
GRUZINSKY PEREULOK
VAL ULITSA
SREDNY TISHINSKY PEREULOK
TISHINSKAYA PLOSHCHAD
BOLSHAYA GRUZINSKAYA ULITSA
TISHINSKY BOL PEREULOK
ULITSA KRASINA
UL GASHEKA
Mayakovskaya
USPENSKY PEREULOK
PETROVSKY BULVAR
KLIMASHKINA ULITSA
GRUZINSKAYA MAL ULITSA
Konsertny Zal Im P I Chaykovskovo
DEGTYARNY PER
TVERSKAYA ULITSA
Tverskaya
Chekhovskaya
STRASTNOY BULVAR
PRESNENSKY
ZOOLOGICHESKAYA UL
SADOVOYE KOLTSO
ERMOLAEVSKY PEREULOK
Pushkinskaya
ULITSA PETROVKA
VOLKOV PER
Zoopark
MALAYA BRONNAYA ULITSA
Patriarshie Prudy
ULITSA SPIRIDONOVKA
BOLSHAYA BRONNAYA UL
TVERSKOY BULVAR
STOLESHNIKOV PER
KRASNAYA PRESNYA ULITSA
Barrikadnaya
VSPOLNY PER
ZAMORENOVA ULITSA
Krasnopresnenskaya
Dom Chekhova
PREDTECHENSKY BOL PER
Kudrinskaya Square Building
KUDRINSKAYA PLOSHCHAD
GRANATNY PER
Dom Maksima Gorkogo
LEONTEVSKY PEREULOK
Moskovskii Khudozhestvennyi Teatr Imeni A Chekhova
KAMERGERSKY PER
Bolshoi Teatr
Teatralnaya
MALAYA NIKITSKAYA ULITSA
BRYUSOV PER
GAZETNY PER
NIKITSKY PER
Okhotny Ryad
ROCHDELSKAYA ULITSA
POVARSKAYA ULITSA
SKATERTNY PEREULOK
BOLSHAYA NIKITSKAYA ULITSA
MERZLYAKOVSKY PER
NIKITSKY BUL
MANEZHNAYA PLOSHCHAD
Kazansky sobor
KONYUSHKOVSKAYA ULITSA
BOL DEVYATINSKY PER EULOK
NOVINSKY BULVAR
TRUBNIKOVSKY PER
Dom Lermontova
Dom Gogolya
MOKHOVAYA UL
Radisson Royal
ULITSA NOVY ARBAT
Arbatskaya
UL VOZDVIZHENKA
Aleksandrovsky Sad
Borovitskaya
Kreml
KUTUZOVSKY PROSPEKT
SHEVCHENKO NAB
TARASA
SMOLENSKAYA NAB
PROTOCHNY PER
KOMPOZITORSKAYA ULITSA
ULITSA ARBAT
STAROKONYUSHENNY PER
AFANASEVSKY PER
GOGOLEVSKY BULVAR
UL ZNAMENKA
Biblioteka Imeni Lenina
Smolenskaya
1-Y SMOLENSKY PER
Dom Pushkina
BORODINSKAYA 2-YA ULITSA
PEREULOK SIVCEV VRAZHEK
KOLYMAZHNAYA ULITSA
ULITSA VOLKHONKA
Ministry of Foreign Affairs
BOLSHOY VLASEVSKY PER
SMOLENSKAYA ULITSA
SMOLENSKAYA-SENNAYA PLOSHCHAD
DENEZHNY PER
PLOTNIKOV PER
GAGARINSKY PEREULOK
Kropotkinskaya
Khram Khrista Spasitela
BOLOTNAYA PLOSHCHAD
Kievskaya
RUZHEYNY PER
PLYUSHCHIKHA ULITSA
BOLSHOY LEVSHINSKY PEREULOK
ULITSA PRECHISTENKA
BERSENEVSKAYA NAB
PRECHISTENSKAYA NABEREZHNAYA
BOLOTNAYA NABEREZHNAYA
Kievsky vokzal
BEREZHKOVSKAYA NABEREZHNAYA
ROSTOVSKAYA NABEREZHNAYA
Moskva
ZEMLEDELCHESKY PER
1-Y NEOPALIMOVSKY PEREULOK
SMOLENSKY BULVAR
KROPOTKINSKY PEREULOK
ULITSA OSTOZHENKA
1-Y ZACHATEVSKY PEREULOK
KOROBEYNIKOV PEREULOK
Tretyakovskaya Galereya
SAVVINSKY BOL PER
ULITSA BURDENKO
ZUBOVSKY BUL
Moscow State University
Park Kultury
KRYMSKAYA NAB
Polyanka

Zemlyanoy Gorod
0
500 metres
0
500 yards
N
Olympiysky
ULITSA DUROVA
Prospekt Mira
6 Botanichesky Sad Mgu
BOL BALKANSKY PEREULOK
GROKHOLSKY PEREULOK
Leningradsky vokzal
Yaroslavsky vokzal
Komsomolskaya
KRASNOPRUDNAYA UL
KRASNOSELSKAYA NIZH UL
ULITSA
OLKHOVSKAYA
MESHCHANSKAYA UL
ULITSA SHCHEPKINA
PROSPEKT MIRA
1 KOPTELSKY PEREULOK
BOLSHAYA SPASSKAYA ULITSA
DOKUCHAEV PER
SKORNYAZHNY PEREULOK
Hilton Hotel Leningradskaya
KALANCHEVSKAYA UL
Kazansky vokzal
RYAZANSKY PROEZD
SADOVOYE KOLTSO
Sukharevskaya
SADOVO-SPASSKAYA UL
PROSPEKT AKADEMIKA SAKHAROVA
NOVORYAZANSKAYA ULITSA
SPARTAKOVSKAYA UL
Baumanskaya
BASMANNY PER
Krasnye Vorota
TRUBNAYA ULITSA
BOL SUKHAREVSKY PEREULOK
BOL GOLOVIN PER
BOL SERGIEVSKY PER
DAEV PEREULOK
UL STRETENKA
LUKOV PER
KOSTYANSKY PEREULOK
Red Gates Administrative Building
KOMMUNY ULITSA
DOBROSLOBODSKAYA
APTEKARSKY PEREULOK
DENISOVSKY PEREULOK
ULITSA
TOKMAKOV PEREULOK
BASMANNY TUPIK
KARLA MARKSA ULITSA
GOROKHOVSKY PER
RADIO ULITSA
ROZHDESTVENSKY BULVAR
Turgenevskaya
MYASNITSKAYA ULITSA
Chistye Prudy
CHISTOPRUDNY BUL
BOLSHOY KHARITONEVSKY PER
FURMANNY PER
ULITSA MASHKOVA
ULITSA CHAPLYGINA
SADOVOYE KOLTSO
BOL KISELNY PER
MILYUTINSKY PER
BOLSHAYA LUBYANKA
KAZAKOVA ULITSA
ULITSA ZEMLYANOY VAL
YELIZAVETINSKY PEREULOK
Kuznetsky Most
UL BOLSHAYA LUBYANKA
Lubyanka
KRIVOKOLENNY PER
POTAPOVSKY PER
ARMYANSKY PER
POKROVKA
BOL KAZENNY PEREULOK
Kurskaya
AKADEMIKA TUPOLEVA NAB
LUBYANSKY PROSPEKT
NOVAYA PL
ULITSA
UL MAROSEYKA
KOLPACHNY PER
KHOKHLOVSKY PER
POKROVSKY BULVAR
LYALIN PEREULOK
PODSOSENSKY PEREULOK
PLOSHCHAD KURSKOGO VOKZALA
Kursky vokzal
Ploshchad Revolyutsii
Kitay-Gorod
STARAYA PLOSHCHAD
ULITSA ILINKA
UL ZABELINA
Chkalovskaya
UL VORONTSOVO POLE
SYROMYATNICHESKAYA NAB
ZOLOTOROZHSKAYA NABEREZHNAYA
Sobor Vasiliya Blazhennovo
UL VARVARKA
Kitay-Gorod
UL SOLYANKA
YAUZSKY BUL
PER OBUKHA
Muzey Sakharova
Palaty Starovo Angliyskovo dvora
PLOSHCHAD YAUZSKIE VOROTA
MOSKVORETSKAYA NAB
Moskva
RAUSHSKAYA NAB
YAUZSKAYA UL
BERNIKOVSKAYA NAB
NIKOLOYAMSKAYA NAB
4
NIKOLOYAMSKAYA ULITSA
Kotelnicheskaya Embankment Building
SADOVNICHESKAYA ULITSA
SADOVNICHESKAYA
OVCHINNIKOVSKAYA NABEREZHNAYA
KOTELNICHESKAYA NAB
TETERINSKY PEREULOK
BOL DROVYANOY PEREULOK
KOMMUNISTICHESKAYA MAL UL
KOMMUNISTICHESKAYA BOLSHAYA ULITSA
ANDRONYEVSKAYA BOL ULITSA
ANDRONYEVSKAYA MAL UL
Rimskaya
ROGOZHSKY VAL ULITSA
ULITSA BOLSHAYA ORDYNKA
Novokuznetskaya
RUNOVSKY PEREULOK
OZERKOVSKAYA NABEREZHNAYA
SADOVNICHESKAYA NABEREZHNAYA
KOSMODAMIANSKAYA NABEREZHNAYA
GONCHARNAYA ULITSA
Taganskaya
TAGANSKAYA PLOSHCHAD
TOVARISHCHESKY PEREULOK
FAKELNY BOL PEREULOK
Marksistskaya
Tretyakovskaya
BOLSHAYA TATARSKAYA ULITSA
2-Y GONCHARNY PER
GONCHARNY PROSP
NARODNAYA UL
Taganskaya
UL MALAYA ORDYNKA
PYATNITSKAYA UL
NOVOKUZNETSKAYA ULITSA
Kolomenskoye

pushing the residents out. The 1980s Arbat was a cosy community of thinkers, artists and writers and the coolest street in the city when compared to the rest of faceless conformist Moscow, but since the fall of Communism much of the authentic atmosphere has been lost, replaced by McDonald's, Hard Rock Cafés and while-u-wait portrait artists. That said, this attractive pedestrian thoroughfare is still a relaxing place to stroll, enjoy a beer or cheap meal in one of the cafés and peruse the souvenir stalls that clutter its length. It still manages to preserve a vibe like no other street in the city and should be on every visitor's itinerary. One of the main 'attractions' on the Arbat is the Peace Wall, plastered with hundreds of tiles painted by Soviet schoolchildren in a regimented propaganda exercise against President Reagan's Star Wars programme. Other back streets leading off the Arbat are daubed in graffiti (the good sort, no tags) with one lane (Krivoarbatsky

Take a break in the café at Patriarshy Pond

pereulok) dedicated to Viktor Tsoy, a cult 1980s rock singer killed in a car accident in 1990. The 1960s poet and songwriter, Bulat Okadzhava, dedicated much of his work to the Arbat and his statue can be found on the corner of Plotnikov pereulok. ⓐ ul. Novy Arbat Ⓜ Metro: Arbatskaya/Smolenskaya

Patriarshie Prudy (Patriarshy Pond)
For a bit of tranquil greenery, head for the Patriarshy Pond, a small body of water in an expensive residential district in the far northwest of the Zemlyanoy Gorod. Some of the action in Bulgakov's *The Master and Margarita* takes place here, and his statue, as well as one of Russian fabulist Ivan Krylov, adorn the park. ⓐ Malaya Bronnaya ul. Ⓜ Metro: Mayakovskaya

Stalinist-era skyscrapers (Seven Sisters)
Five of the so-called Seven Sisters, monolithic Stalinist-era skyscrapers, lie on or very near the Garden Ring Road. These impressive Gotham-city-style towers were built in the late 1940s and 1950s to make Moscow appear a bit more like a major city after the war. Nine were planned but only seven actually built. Love them or hate them, these neo-Gothic monsters are probably here to stay.

Starting in the west, the **Ministry of Foreign Affairs** (ⓐ Smolenskaya-Sennaya pl. 32/34 Ⓜ Metro: Smolenskaya) is 172 m (564 ft) tall and can be seen from the Arbat. Further north rises the **Kudrinskaya Square Building** (ⓐ Kudrinskaya pl. 1 Ⓜ Metro: Barrikadnaya) at 160 m (525 ft), and just across the Moskva River towers the **Hotel Radisson Royal** (ⓐ Kutuzovsky pl. 2/1 Ⓜ Metro: Kievskaya), the second-tallest sister at 198 m (650 ft). In the east, the **Hotel Hilton Leningraskaya** (ⓐ Kalantchevskaya 21/40

Metro: Komsomolskaya), which hits 136 m (446 ft), and the 133m (436 ft) **Red Gates Administrative Building** (Sadovo-Spasskaya 21 Metro: Krasnye Vorota) stand just a few hundred metres apart. The two remaining sisters are the **Kotelnicheskaya Embankment Building** (Kotelnitcheskaya nab. 1/15 Metro: Kitay-Gorod), which looms 176 m (577 ft) high above the confluence of the Moskva and Yauza rivers, and the **Moscow State University** (Vorobievy Gori Metro: Universitet), the tallest tower at 240 m (787 ft).

CULTURE

Kolomenskoye

A beautiful park and museum complex consisting of no less than 17 monuments and recognised as a UNESCO World Heritage Site. Twelve of the buildings were constructed on this site between the 16th and 19th centuries as part of an ever-expanding imperial estate, while others are wooden constructions brought in from different regions of Russia to form an open-air museum. As well as exhibitions in several of the buildings there are various tours, concerts, boat cruises and horse and carriage rides on offer; the events programme varies throughout the year so call for details. All in all a fascinating place to spend the day. pr. Andropova 39 499 612 2768 http://mgomz.com Complex: 07.00–22.00 Apr–Oct; 08.00–21.00 Nov–Mar; museums: 10.00–18.00 Metro: Kolomenskaya

Konsertny Zal Im. P I Chaykovskovo (Tchaikovsky Concert Hall)

Home to the State Philharmonic Orchestra, this huge auditorium

The Ministry of Foreign Affairs

which can accommodate audiences of almost 1,600 is one of the best classical music venues in the city. Tickets don't cost

HOUSE MUSEUMS

The former homes of some of the biggest names in Russian literature have been transformed into museums containing original manuscripts, personal objects and other items relating to their lives and their works.

Dom Chekhova (Chekhov House) ⓐ ul. Sadovaya-Kudrinskaya 6, off Sadovoye Koltso ⓣ (495) 691 3837 ⓛ 11.00–18.00 Tues, Thur, Sun, 14.00–20.00 Wed, Fri ⓜ Metro: Barrikadnaya. Admission charge

Dom Gogolya (Gogol House) ⓐ Nikitsky bul. 7A ⓣ (495) 691 1550 ⓦ www.domgogolya.ru ⓛ 12.00–19.00 Mon, Wed–Fri, 12.00–17.00 Sat & Sun ⓜ Metro: Arbatskaya. Admission charge

Dom Maksima Gorkogo (Gorky House) ⓐ Malaya Nikitskaya ul. 6/2 ⓣ (495) 690 0535 ⓛ 11.00–17.30 Wed–Sun ⓜ Metro: Arbatskaya ⓘ Closed last Thur of month

Dom Lermontova (Lermontov House) ⓐ ul. Malaya Molchanovka 2, near ul. Novy Arbat ⓣ (495) 691 5298 ⓛ 14.00–18.00 Wed, Fri, 11.00–17.00 Thur, Sat & Sun ⓜ Metro: Arbatskaya. Admission charge ⓘ Closed last day of month

Dom Pushkina (Pushkin House) ⓐ ul. Arbat 53 ⓐ (499) 241 4212 ⓛ 10.00–18.00 Wed–Sun ⓜ Metro: Smolenskaya. Admission charge

a packet and the standard of performance is extremely high. ⓐ Triumfalnaya pl. 4/13 ⓣ (495) 232 0400 ⓦ www.classicalmusic.ru Metro: Mayakovskaya

Muzey Sakharova (Sakharov Museum)

The centre containing a library and superb exhibitions on the *gulag*, the dissident movement and Soviet repression (including recent images from Chechnya), was built in memory of Andrei Sakharov. Few in the USSR were more outspoken or critical of the Soviet system than Sakharov, who began as a Soviet physicist on the USSR's top-secret nuclear weapons project in the 1950s and is known as the creator of the Soviet H-bomb. In the 1960s he became a critic of the Soviet system and a leading dissident who campaigned for improvements in human rights and against nuclear weapons. He won the Nobel Peace Prize in 1975 but was banished to Gorky in 1980 after criticising the Soviet invasion of Afghanistan. Hounded by the KGB and forbidden to travel in the early 1980s, he was eventually invited to join the *perestroika* government of Mikhail Gorbachev in 1986 and drafted a new constitution shortly before his death in 1989.

Appropriately, the museum that bears his name comes under pressure from the Church and government for its controversial stance. ⓐ ul. Zemlyanoy Val 57/6 ⓣ (495) 623 4401 ⓦ www.sakharov-museum.ru 11.00–19.00 Tues–Sun Metro: Kurskaya or Chkalovskaya

Novaya Opera (New Opera)

Founded as recently as 1991 by Russian conductor Evgeny Kolobov and Moscow Mayor Yuri Luzhkov, the New Opera hosts the widest possible range of classical opera and ballet and is regarded as one of the best opera houses in Russia. ⓐ ul. Karetny Ryad 3/2 (Hermitage Gardens) ⓣ (495) 694 0868 ⓦ www.novayaopera.ru ⓜ Metro: Chekhovskaya, Tverskaya or Pushkinskaya

RETAIL THERAPY

Arbat Street The souvenir stalls on the Arbat are one of the best places to buy *matryoshka* dolls, Red Army memorabilia (though much of this is now made-in-China imitation), postcards, artwork and general bric-à-brac left over from the Soviet days.

Arbatskaya Lavitsa Whether it's a Russian doll, brightly coloured lacquer work or a richly decorated *samovar* you are after, Lavitsa has the largest selection of typical Russian souvenirs on Arbat Street and there's no hard sell, unlike on the street stalls outside. ⓐ ul. Arbat 27 ⓣ (495) 690 4669 ⓛ 09.00–21.00 ⓜ Metro: Smolenskaya

Atrium Standing almost opposite the Kursky railway station, this large shopping centre is not as exclusive as others in the city centre and has a wide selection of stores. ⓐ ul. Zemlyanoy Val 33 ⓣ (495) 970 1555 ⓛ 11.00–23.00 ⓜ Metro: Kurskaya or Chkalovskaya

TAKING A BREAK

Kruzhka £ ❶ With most dishes costing around 250RUR and beer going for 50RUR a pint, it's not surprising this chain of cheap eateries has become a refuge for students and cash-strapped travellers.

ⓐ Kudrinskaya pl. 1 ⓣ (499) 252 1068 ⓦ www.kruzhka.com ⓒ 12.00–00.00 Sun–Thur, 12.00–04.00 Fri & Sat ⓜ Metro: Barrikadnaya

Moo Moo £ ❷ Similar to the Soviet milk bars of yore, Moo Moo is a self-service cheap eat with branches across the city. This one is in a perfect location on the busy Arbat and hits the spot every time with its large portions and English menus. ⓐ ul. Arbat 45/1 ⓣ (499) 241 1364 ⓒ 10.00–23.00 ⓜ Metro: Smolenskaya

Yolki Palki ££ ❸ Traditional Russian eatery with a rustic theme. ⓐ ul. Novy Arbat 11/1 ⓣ (495) 691 7654 ⓒ 11.00–00.00 ⓜ Metro: Arbatskaya

AFTER DARK

RESTAURANTS

Baklazhan £ ❹ If Moscow's Georgian restaurants seem too expensive or too fancy, try this tiny no-frills version with its brightly decorated ceiling, big portions, low prices and simple interior. ⓐ Nikoloyamskaya ul.29 ⓣ (495) 915 3313 ⓒ 11.00–23.00 ⓜ Metro: Taganskaya

Shesh-Besh ££ ❺ Not to be confused with Kishmish, an Uzbek eatery in the same street, Shesh-Besh is an inexpensive Azeri restaurant serving filling dishes including legendary *shashlyk* (kebab) and an excellent value lunch buffet. ⓐ ul. Novy Arbat 24/2 ⓣ (495) 690 1922 ⓦ www.rmcom.ru ⓒ 12.00–00.00 ⓜ Metro: Arbatskaya

Kavkazkaya Plennitsa £££ ❻ The name of this Georgian restaurant just north of the Garden Ring Road means 'Caucasus Prisoner' and it will certainly captivate you with Georgian favourites such as *lobio* (bean salad), *satsivi* (chicken with walnut sauce) and *hachapuri* (cheese pie). ⓐ pr. Mira 36 ⓣ (495) 680 5177 🕒 12.00–00.00 Ⓜ Metro: Prospekt Mira

Tiflis £££ ❼ No ordinary Georgian dive but an upmarket island of Caucasian culture: ingredients and wine are sourced in Georgia and the eight elegant dining spaces are reminiscent of the country's capital. ⓐ ul. Ostozhenka 32 ⓣ (499) 766 9728 ⓦ www.tiflis.ru 🕒 12.00–00.00 Ⓜ Metro: Park Kultury

CLUBS

Ikra Club Immensely popular with young clubbers for its DJ sets, pumping music and live concerts. ⓐ ul. Kazakova 8a ⓣ (495) 729 3628 ⓦ www.ikraclub.ru 🕒 12.00–07.00 Ⓜ Metro: Kurskaya

Night Flight Get past face control and you're in for a taste of the city's seedier side at Moscow's original late-night venue, established in 1991. Although relatively tame in its 'entertainment' programme, beware any unsolicited female advances here. Join the crowd of lonely business travellers, spending their company's cash, for a flute of Dom Perignon, then retire to the Cigar Lounge or dance until dawn on the seething dance floor. ⓐ Tverskaya ul. 17 ⓣ (495) 629 4165 ⓦ www.nightflight.ru 🕒 Restaurant: 18.00–04.00; club: 20.00–05.00 Ⓜ Metro: Pushkinskaya, Tverskaya or Chekhovskaya

---

▶ *Sergiev Posad's domes sparkle on a summer's day*

OUT OF TOWN
trips

Suzdal

Suzdal is one of the highlights of the so-called Golden Ring, a group of historical towns to the northeast of Moscow. Lying some 200 km (124 miles) from the capital, this small town is a wonderfully picturesque place of fortified monasteries, onion domes and fairytale timber houses strung along the romantically meandering Kamenka River. With its tranquil monasteries, reedy river banks and slow pace of life, Suzdal is the perfect antidote to Moscow's neon lights, choking pollution and tasteless extravagance. But don't be fooled by its present-day torpor – this was once the medieval capital of a fledgling Russian state and a major religious centre.

A village first appeared on the banks of the lazy River Kamenka in the early 11th century, and within a century Yury Dolgoruky, builder of the first Moscow Kremlin, had declared Suzdal his capital. In 1157 top-dog status was transferred to nearby Vladimir but Suzdal remained an important trading centre. Annexed by Moscow in 1392, over the next 400 years Suzdal became a focal point for the Orthodox Church, and at one time boasted 50 churches and more than ten monasteries. Although many of these were closed during Communist rule (12 churches were even destroyed), Suzdal still has an incredible five monasteries and a church seemingly on every street corner. This town of just 11,000 souls boasts an amazing 314 historical sights, some of which have made it onto UNESCO's list of World Heritage Sites. Ulitsa Lenina runs north–south the entire length of the town and links up all

A unique bell tower with clock

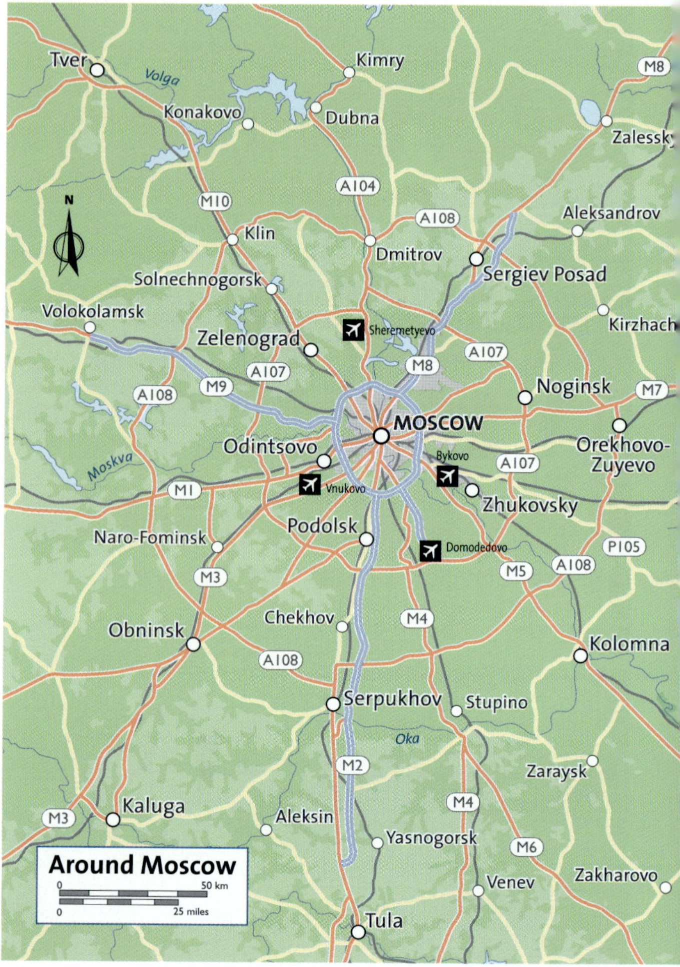
Around Moscow
0
50 km
0
25 miles
N
Tver
Volga
Kimry
M8
Konakovo
Dubna
Zalessky
A104
M10
A108
Aleksandrov
Klin
Dmitrov
Sergiev Posad
Solnechnogorsk
Volokolamsk
Kirzhach
Sheremetyevo
Zelenograd
A107
M8
A107
Noginsk
M7
M9
A108
MOSCOW
Orekhovo-Zuyevo
Odintsovo
Bykovo
A107
Moskva
Vnukovo
Zhukovsky
M1
Podolsk
Naro-Fominsk
Domodedovo
P105
A108
M5
M3
Chekhov
M4
Obninsk
Kolomna
A108
Serpukhov
Stupino
Oka
M2
Zaraysk
M4
Kaluga
M3
Aleksin
Yasnogorsk
M6
Zakharovo
Venev
Tula

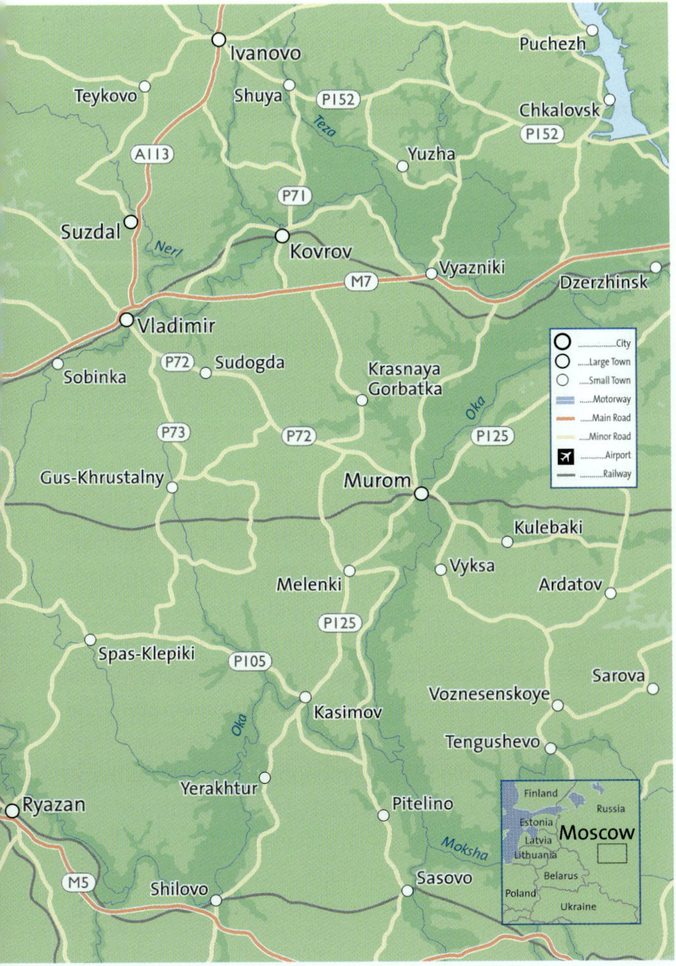
Ivanovo
Puchezh
Teykovo
Shuya
P152
Teza
Chkalovsk
P152
A113
Yuzha
P71
Suzdal
Nerl
Kovrov
Vyazniki
M7
Dzerzhinsk
Vladimir
City
Large Town
Small Town
Motorway
Main Road
Minor Road
Airport
Railway
Sobinka
P72
Sudogda
Krasnaya
Gorbatka
Oka
P73
P72
P125
Gus-Khrustalny
Murom
Kulebaki
Vyksa
Melenki
Ardatov
P125
Spas-Klepiki
P105
Sarova
Voznesenskoye
Kasimov
Oka
Tengushevo
Yerakhtur
Finland
Russia
Ryazan
Pitelino
Estonia
Moscow
Latvia
Lithuania
Moksha
Belarus
M5
Shilovo
Sasovo
Poland
Ukraine

the places of interest. The winding Kamenka River flows slowly to the west and can be crossed using wooden footbridges. Suzdal is only just feasible as a day trip and an overnight stay will make things much simpler.

GETTING THERE

By rail & road

Only one bus per day travels between Moscow's main Shchyolkovsky bus station and Suzdal. If you miss this, take a bus or train to Vladimir, from where there is a half-hourly bus service to Suzdal.

SIGHTS & ATTRACTIONS

Kreml (Kremlin)

Suzdal's Kremlin has occupied a bend in the river in the town's southern reaches since the 12th century. The complex of ramparts, churches and palace buildings is one of the main draws in Suzdal and the place where most people begin their exploration of the town. The Cathedral of the Nativity is rarely open to the public but is impressive enough from the outside, with its snowy white façade and its blue onion domes dusted with golden stars. The adjacent Archbishop's Palace houses a museum and the Cross Chamber, where you may be lucky enough to catch a performance by a local choir. Opposite the palace, the timber Church of St Nicholas, with its ancient log structure and steep wooden slat roof, originally stood in the village of Glotovo but was moved here in 1950. Grounds: 24 hrs; museums: 10.00–18.00 Wed–Mon Closed last Fri of month

Cathedral of the Nativity beside the Archbishop's Palace

OTHER PLACES OF INTEREST

Suzdal is rich in sights and attractions. The Convent of the Intercession on the east bank of the river has another cathedral and museum. The convent used to serve as a place unwanted tsars' wives were exiled from Moscow. There's also a good little restaurant in the refectory and a small museum. The Trading Rows to the north of the local Kremlin is where merchants used to do business, and north of that lies another convent called the Deposition of the Robes, boasting yet another cathedral. Churches line ulitsa Kremlyovskaya and ulitsa Lenina from the Kremlin to the convent and there are numerous churches dotted around the town for visitors to discover.

Spaso-Yevfimiev monastyr (Saviour Monastery of St Euphimius)
Founded in 1352 and once one of the wealthiest monasteries in all Russia, the complex served as a prison during the reign of Catherine the Great and as a POW camp for Nazi soldiers during World War II. The Cathedral of the Transfiguration is topped with five delightful green onion domes and the interior holds some valuable frescoes. The Museum of Treasures has a collection of impressive icons and the Museum of Naïve Art housed in a deconsecrated church displays early 19th-century paintings with a rural theme. Another exhibition deals with the monastery's role as a World War II POW camp. ⓐ ul. Lenina ◷ 10.00–18.00 Tues–Sun ⓘ Closed last Thur of month. Admission charge

CULTURE

Kupala
A pagan festival in early July which involves lots of bonfire leaping, naked night-time bathing among the reeds of the Kamenka River and much vodka-induced frolicking. Just turn up and join in. A fabulous way to make friends you never need to meet again, once you've sobered up.

Muzey Derevyannovo Zodchestva (Museum of Timber Architecture)
One commodity there's no shortage of in Russia is wood, and this is demonstrated at the town's open-air museum, where just about everything is made of the stuff. The museum has gathered together fine examples of rural timber architecture

◗ *The wooden churches of Suzdal*

SUZDAL CUCUMBER FESTIVAL

To the Russian mind in general and the Suzdalian in particular, the cucumber has connotations far more noble than the ones it conjures in the post-Freudian Western mind. In Suzdal, the cucumber is no sniggering matter. As the new potato is to Jersey and gateau is to the Black Forest, so the cucumber is to Suzdal. Here, it is a dietary staple (and has been for at least 500 years, since its importation from India), with locals using it to make soups, cakes and even wine. There are at least a hundred different varieties – as opposed to the crude Western division into cucumber, gherkin and – at a stretch – courgette. It's even a key component of a local saying that warns against the folly of making comparisons between disparate phenomena (it translates roughly as 'don't compare a five-kopeck coin to a salted cucumber', but must be snappier in the Russian).

Suzdal is known for the quality of its bendy green veg, and it is said that every household in the town and surrounding countryside grows them. Thus it is not so surprising that every July in Suzdal heralds the **Cucumber Festival** (see Ⓦ www.museum.vladimir.ru for exact dates and details). Although the creeping plant is its undisputed focus – at this time of the year, houses are strewn with their effigies, and some people even dress up as vegetables – it has expanded its scope to celebrate local folk culture in general, with musical events, craft shows and lectures on

> cookery and the folk legends of Prince Cucumber (a variation on the Green Man cycle-of-growth figure). In this republic, cucumber is king. The average man in the street in Suzdal wouldn't give a fig for your Knighthood or your Congressional Gold Medal: around here, the hope of being recognised as having the town's biggest cucumber is what drives people on.

from surrounding buildings and renovated them for posterity. Guides in folk costume are mines of information on the various churches, farm buildings, cabins, watermills and windmills on the site. ⓐ ul. Pushkarskaya ⓛ 09.00–19.00 ⓘ Closed last day of month. Admission charge

RETAIL THERAPY

Unless you're after a bottle or two of *medovukha* (see below), some religious icons or an Orthodox bible, you're not likely to go on a spending spree in Suzdal. The gift shop at the open-air museum stocks some souvenir material.

TAKING A BREAK

Apart from cucumbers, Suzdal is also known for its *medovukha*, a cider-like brew made from honey. Give it a try, you might even like it!

Slavyansky Bar £ A low-cost bar and café at the Kremlin where

The comfortable Hotel Pushkarskaya Sloboda

you can get a meal and a beer for Russian countryside prices. ⓐ ul. Kremlyovskaya 6 ⓣ (49231) 20 062 ⓛ 10.00–01.00

Kremlin Trapeznaya ££ It's claimed that this medieval refectory has been serving hearty Russian fare for 300 years! A grand affair within the Archbishop's Palace. ⓐ Suzdal Kremlin ⓣ (49231) 21 763 ⓦ www.trapeznaya.ru ⓛ 11.00–23.00

ACCOMMODATION

It's advisable to book accommodation in advance, especially in the summer months, around New Year and during the Kupala and Cucumber festivals (see pages 112 & 114).

Hotel Pushkarskaya Sloboda ££ A relatively upmarket place, with classic hotel rooms in a renovated 19th-century main building and a complex of timber cabins which are used in summer. Breakfast not included. ⓐ ul. Lenina 45 ⓣ (49231) 23 303 ⓦ www.sloboda-gk.ru

Vishnevy Sad (Cherry Garden) ££ A small hotel in Suzdal's historic centre on the Mzhara river bank. The interior replicates the typical house of a wealthy merchant in the 19th century. ⓐ ul. Lenina 10 ⓣ (49231) 23 246 ⓦ www.cherrygarden.ru

Nicholaevsky Posad ££–£££ A new hotel complex of eight townhouses in the very heart of Suzdal. Among the complex's facilities is a restaurant, Kupechesky. ⓐ ul. Lenina 138 ⓣ (49231) 23 585 ⓦ www.nposad.ru

Sergiev Posad

The town of Sergiev Posad, 60 km (37 miles) north of the capital, is home to Russia's finest, holiest and most important monastery, the Troitse-Sergeyeva lavra (see page 122), and constitutes the most popular day trip visitors make from Moscow. The town itself is a grey product of the post-Soviet years, but at its heart is a complex of religious buildings which is stunning to behold. Now, many may consider several hours walking around a monastery town a relaxing though not particularly interesting experience, but Sergiev Posad is different. Its ensemble of churches, ramparts, towers and gardens assault the senses with their colour and fairytale decoration; huge bulbous onion domes in gold and star-sprinkled azure seem unreal (even close up), and the richly decorated interiors of the many places of worship with their frescoes, icons, tiled floors and painted ceilings almost overwhelm the visitor in a riot of colour. This is Orthodox religious architecture at its very best and should not be missed. Even the tsars made a pilgrimage here – on foot!

The monastery was founded by a hermit monk, St Sergius of Radonezh, patron saint of Russia (see page 120), and his brother Stephen in 1340. The tiny monastery began attracting people escaping from the Mongols who occupied Russia's cities. Under Tsar Ivan the Terrible the monastery gained its defensive walls and towers, and up until 1917 it grew in size and stature as a major place of pilgrimage. The Bolsheviks banished the monks

The enormous bell tower in the Trinity Monastery

to Siberia in 1920 and renamed the town Zagorsk, but Stalin allowed the monastery to reopen in the early 1950s in gratitude for the Orthodox Church's support during World War II.

Convenient and frequent transport options between the capital and Sergiev Posad make this an easy day or half-day excursion, and people rarely stay over night. What's more, admission to the grounds is free, though there's a small charge for taking photographs (which you'll most certainly want to). The best time to visit is from Tuesday to Friday as the museums close on Mondays and the churches at weekends.

THE UNORTHODOX ORTHODOX SAINT

You might think that a life that included playing a decisive role in Russian military history and founding the Trinity Monastery of St Sergius (see page 122) suggests a certain amount of drive; and that to have a posthumous CV that includes being made a national saint implies a degree of ambition. In the case of Sergius of Radonezh, you'd be absolutely right; but Sergius was a total failure, as his only ambition was complete obscurity.

Born to a wealthy family some time in the early 1320s, from a young age Sergius had no interest in anything wordly. His wish was to live a life of asceticism, in order to rid himself of ego and thus, in his view, bring himself closer to God. To this end, he went to live alone in a forest just outside what is now Sergiev Posad. After a couple of years, gossip about the hermit in the woods attracted

GETTING THERE

By rail & road

Pilgrims used to take a week to reach Sergiev Posad; for you the journey from Moscow should be much less time consuming. Half-hourly suburban elektrichki (commuter trains) run from the city's Yaroslavsky Station (see page 49), taking 90 minutes to cover the 60 km (37 miles), and buses operate with the same frequency from the VDNKH metro station, reaching Sergiev Posad in around an hour.

people's attention and, as his belief system demanded that he do what others wished of him, Sergius acknowledged this attention, and a group of what we would call Orthodox Christians gathered around him. (He only founded the Trinity Monastery so that they would have somewhere to live.) Word spread further about this impressively religious man, and he became such a popular figure that he was asked to bless the Russian forces before the battle of Kulikovo in 1380 (see page 14). Russian success in that battle was credited to Sergius, and he became a national superstar. He spent the rest of his life blessing people and solving disputes, because that's what was asked of him. In 1452, 60 years after his death, Sergius was made patron saint of Russia – a paradoxical achievement for a man who wanted only to forget himself, and to be forgotten.

SIGHTS & ATTRACTIONS

Troitse-Sergeyeva lavra (Trinity Monastery of St Sergius)

The following describes a clockwise walk around the grounds of this glorious, huge monastery. Having entered through the Red Tower in the eastern wall, the first building you encounter is the Gateway Church of St John the Baptist, with its red-and-white walls and modest cupolas. To the left stands the colourful Refectory Church of St Sergius, with every inch of its walls decorated lavishly, its columns entwined with painted vines and the interior a confusion of gold ornament and frescoed ceiling. The miniature Church of St Mica stands right by its side. Across the path from the refectory sits the Church of the Descent of the Holy Spirit, sporting a single blue onion dome. Behind that is the late 16th-century Dormition Cathedral, with its four bright blue cupolas dusted with gold leaf stars and gathered around a central gilt dome. All five are topped with huge orthodox crosses. The real religious heart of the monastery, however, is the Trinity Cathedral which can be found on the western perimeter. This Byzantine structure dates from 1422, but stands on the site of the original church from the time of St Sergius (see page 120). The dark interior, lit only by oil lamps which cast a dim light on radiant icons, hosts a service which continues all day, every day. The cathedral is usually full of pilgrims who have come to see the silver shrine containing the relics of St Sergius. Next door is a museum packed with icons and royal portraits. From here, walk north past the huge, five-tiered baroque bell tower to the rotund Church of the Virgin of Smolensk, the Church of St Zosima and the green Pilgrim's Gate. In front of the gate extends the Tsar's Palace, which now houses a seminary.

The Dormition Cathedral

The walls encircling the *lavra* are supported by towers at each corner. The most interesting is the so-called Duck Tower, which got its name after Peter the Great used it as a vantage point from which to shoot the poor creatures. (496) 540 5721 Complex: 05.00–21.00 (24 hrs 18 July–8 Sept); museum: 10.00–17.30 Tues–Sun. Admission charge for museum (complex free)

Muzey Igrushki (Toy Museum)
This relatively impressive museum houses exhibitions of toys from Russia and around the world, reflecting the town's toy-making tradition. pr. Krasnoy Armii 15 (49654) 44 101 10.00–17.00 Wed–Sun Closed last Fri of month. Admission charge

RETAIL THERAPY

Thanks to the number of visitors the monastery receives, a large group of stalls selling souvenirs and traditional handicrafts is a permanent fixture in the grounds.

TAKING A BREAK

Should you have trouble finding somewhere to eat in Sergiev Posad, try one of these touristy restaurants near the monastery:
Russky Dvorik ££ pr. Krasnoy Armii 134/2 (49654) 05 114 www.russky-dvorik-restaurant.ru 10.00–21.00
Traktir 'Pechki & Lavochki' ££ ul. Mit'kina 14/2 (496) 547 5392 07.00–00.00

The art train at Kievskaya Metro station

PRACTICAL information

Directory

GETTING THERE

By air

The city is well-served by major flag carriers and a handful of budget airlines. From the UK, British Airways, Aeroflot, BMI and Transaero all operate direct flights to Moscow and many other national airlines such as **Swiss** (ⓦ www.swiss.com), **Czech Airlines** (ⓦ www.czechairlines.com), **LOT** (ⓦ www.lot.com), **SAS** (ⓦ www.flysas.com), **Lufthansa** (ⓦ www.lufthansa.com), **Malev** (ⓦ www.malev.com) and **Alitalia** (ⓦ www.alitalia.com) fly to Russia via hubs in their home countries. As yet, no budget airline flies direct from the UK to Moscow but savvy travellers are taking no-frills flights from London and regional airports to places like Berlin and Riga, where they can change onto local low-cost carriers such as Germanwings, Air Berlin and airBaltic for the final leg. This is the best option for visitors from North America, Australia and New Zealand.

Aeroflot Heathrow to Sheremetyevo 2 ⓦ www.aeroflot.com

Air Berlin Many airports across Germany to Domodedovo Airport ⓦ www.airberlin.com

airBaltic Riga to Sheremetyevo 2 ⓦ www.airbaltic.com

BMI Flights to Domodedovo Airport ⓦ www.flybmi.com

British Airways Heathrow to Domodedovo Airport ⓦ www.ba.com

Germanwings Berlin-Schönefeld to Vnukovo Airport ⓦ www.germanwings.com

Transaero Heathrow to Domodedovo Airport ⓦ www.transaero.com

Many people are aware that air travel emits CO_2, which contributes to climate change. You may be interested in the possibility of lessening the environmental impact of your flight through **Climate Care** (w www.climatecare.org), which offsets your CO_2 by funding environmental projects around the world.

By rail

If you do decide to attempt the London–Moscow journey by train, hop on the **Eurostar** (w www.eurostar.com) to Brussels, change onto an express to Cologne and then take a sleeper to Moscow. The whole journey takes two to three days. For up-to-date train timetables, consult the ***Thomas Cook European Rail Timetable and Overseas Timetable*** (t (UK) 01733 416 477 w www.thomascookpublishing.com).

The spacious waiting lounge at Domodedovo Airport

By road

It is possible to travel to Moscow by coach, but this can take over two days. Ecolines operates coaches from London to Riga and Riga to Moscow. However, taking a budget flight to Riga and then the coach works out cheaper (even if it can be a bit of a nuisance transferring from plane to coach), and makes for a considerably shorter journey.

Ecolines ⓦ www.ecolines.net

ENTRY FORMALITIES

Every foreigner requires a visa. There are basically three types – private, business and tourist. For short breaks to Moscow, a 30-day tourist visa is the best option. If you are travelling to Russia as part of an organised tour, your travel agent or tour operator will look after the visa application for you. Independent travellers should use a reputable visa agency. The following are tried and tested:

Alpha-Omega Travel ⓐ 16 Eldon Place, Bradford, West Yorkshire BD1 3AZ ⓣ (01274) 760 600 ⓦ www.alpha-omega.ru

Real Russia ⓐ 3 The Ivories, Northampton Street, Islington, London N1 2HY ⓣ (020) 7100 7370 ⓦ www.realrussia.co.uk

Zierer Visa Service ⓐ 60 East 42nd Street, Suite 1250, New York, NY 10165 ⓣ 866 788 1100 ⓦ www.zvs.com ❗ Other offices in Houston, San Francisco, Washington, Europe and Australia

Once in Russia, you must officially register your visa. If you are staying at a hotel, reception staff will do this for you. Otherwise you must go through the process yourself. Agencies such as Real Russia have sister companies in Moscow that can complete the process for a fee. Failure to register your visa can lead to you being fined by the police.

MONEY

The currency in Russia is the rouble (RUR), which is divided into 100 kopecks. Notes come in denominations of 10, 50, 100, 500, 1,000 and 5,000 roubles, and coins in denominations of 1, 10 and 50 kopecks and 1, 2, 5 and 10 roubles. To find out the current exchange rate, visit ⓦ www.xe.com.

ATMs are as common in Moscow as they are in any Western city. On-screen instructions can usually be viewed in English and machines sometimes give the option of making withdrawals in US dollars. Tell your bank or credit card company you intend making transactions in Russia.

Pounds sterling, euros and US dollars can be changed at banks and small kiosks such as the ubiquitous **Sberbank** (ⓦ www.sbrf.ru). Make sure all foreign notes are in good order as cashiers will refuse them if they're shabby. Avoid the banks' high transaction fees by using credit cards or withdrawing cash from ATMs.

Tips are always welcome. In cheap and middle-of-the-road eateries round the bill up to the nearest 50 or 100RUR. In more upmarket restaurants you may want to tip bigger. Tour guides should always be tipped. Taxi drivers from official companies also appreciate a bit extra on top of the bill. Tips can be given in roubles, dollars or euros, though British pounds are not always welcome.

HEALTH, SAFETY & CRIME

Your main crime concern should be petty theft, which is common in crowded places, particularly on the metro. Always carry a photocopy of your passport (never the real thing), and if a policeman insists there is a problem with your papers, ask to be taken to the nearest police station. Getting a passer-by (witness) to translate is also a good idea. Racism is a big problem in today's Russia and those from ethnic minorities should take extra care. Usually Muscovites will just stare, but occasionally things can get nasty. Three-lane highways cut across the city and should only be crossed at subways or metro stations. Driving standards in Russia can be abysmal, so do be careful.

OPENING HOURS

Every business must, by law, display their trading hours on the door or window of their premises. Opening times are pretty rigid and premises in general open and close when they should. However, be aware that many offices and businesses take an hour's break for lunch.

Most attractions open at 09.00 or 10.00 and close around 17.00 or 18.00. They usually close on one day a week. Banks are open 09.00–18.00 Monday to Friday, with some central banks open on Saturdays too. Many shops are open every day of the week between 10.00–20.00, although a few still close on Sundays. A few grocery stores conveniently remain open around the clock.

TOILETS

Russia doesn't really do public toilets, and anything you do chance upon will be pretty grimy. In recent years rows of blue plastic portaloos have sprung up at convenient places such as in front of railway stations, at markets etc, but you'll find none in the very centre of the city. Facilities at restaurants, cafés, railway stations, shopping centres and museums all come in handy, though at stations spending a penny will probably cost you around 15–25RUR.

CHILDREN

Moscow is not the best holiday destination for children. Extremes of temperature in summer and winter, pollution, crowds, killer roads and a general lack of facilities are bad news for families. To entertain the wee ones in comfort and safety, head for Gorky Park (see page 65), where there are rides in summer and an ice rink in winter, the Alexandrovsky Gardens (see page 64), where you will find several playgrounds, or the **Matryoshka Museum** (ⓐ Leontevsky per. 7 ⓣ (495) 691 7556 ◷ 10.00–18.00 Mon–Thur, 10.00–17.00 Fri & Sat Ⓜ Metro: Okhotny Ryad).

Children love the circus and Moscow has more than one: the most central is **Nikulin Circus** (ⓐ Tsvetnoy bul. 13 ⓣ (495) 625 8970 ⓦ www.circusnikulin.ru Ⓜ Metro: Tsvetnoy Bulvar). Or why not try one of the city's children's theatres? Little ones will have many a giggle at **Obraztsov Puppet Theatre** (ⓐ Sadovaya-Samotechnaya ul. 3 ⓣ (495) 699 5373 ⓦ www.puppet.ru Ⓜ Metro: Tsvetnoy Bulvar) and won't worry about the language difference in the dramas put on at **Natalya Sats Moscow Children's Theatre** (ⓐ pr. Vernadskovo 5 ⓣ (495) 930 7021 ⓦ www.teatr-sats.ru Ⓜ Metro: Universitet).

COMMUNICATIONS

Internet

The number of Wi-Fi hotspots is on the increase in central Moscow, with many more upmarket restaurants, cafés and hotels facilitating access. The **Beeline** Wi-Fi network (ⓦ http://wifi.beeline.ru) covers the whole city. If you aren't travelling with your own laptop, head to one of Moscow's many internet cafés. Two of the best are:

Cofemax ⓐ ul. Pyatnitskaya 25/1 ⓣ (495) 950 6050 ⓦ http://cofemax.cafemax.ru ⓛ 24 hrs

MDM Internet Centre ⓐ Komsomolsky pr. 28 ⓣ (495) 782 8839 ⓦ http://mdm-internet.ru ⓛ 24 hrs

Phone

Payphones are widespread in Moscow. To use one, you must obtain a prepaid card from a kiosk. Phone cards from other cities in Russia will not work in the capital.

TELEPHONING RUSSIA

The country code for Russia is 7 and the code for Moscow is either 495 or 499. To ring a number in Moscow from abroad, use your country's international dialling code (00 from the UK, 001 from the US), followed by 7, followed by 495 or 499 as appropriate and the local seven-digit number.

TELEPHONING ABROAD

To make an international call from Russia, dial 8, wait for a second tone then dial 10 plus the country code (UK 44, US & Canada 1, Ireland 353), area code and local number.

Even if you are able to use your mobile phone while in Moscow, making and receiving calls will be very expensive. If you're staying longer than a few days, consider buying a Russian SIM card from operators such as MTS, Beeline or Megafon. SIM cards are available from **Euroset** (t (495) 777 7710) or **Svyaznoy** (t (495) 500 0333 w www.svyaznoy.ru), which have outlets all over the city and at the entrance to most metro stations.

Post

The post office is run by Pochta Rossii and branches are easily recognisable by a dark blue sign bearing the words Почта России and the Russian double-headed eagle holding a post horn in each talon. Moscow's **main post office** (a Myasnitskaya 26 24 hrs Metro: Chistye Prudy or Turgenevskaya) can be found to the northwest of Red Square on the first ring road. You'll pay 19RUR

Sign for the post office

to send a postcard airmail to another country and 22.50RUR for a letter weighing less than 20 g. Letters and postcards take around three weeks to the UK and up to a month to reach addresses on other continents. The Russian postal system has seen a huge improvement in recent years and your postcards home are now very unlikely to go astray (unlike much incoming mail). For further information, see ⓦ www.russianpost.ru.

ELECTRICITY

Russia works on 220V AC, 50Hz. To use electrical appliances from home you will need a continental two-pin adaptor.

TRAVELLERS WITH DISABILITIES

Unfortunately, Moscow still has a long way to go in terms of providing accessible facilities for wheelchair users and people with other disabilities. Ramps and lifts are almost non-existent on public transport and many tourist attractions are inaccessible to those who cannot manage steps. Some Western chain hotels offer adapted rooms and bathrooms, but make sure you search around and obtain definite confirmation of their facilities before booking anything.

The following organisations may be able to provide advice or useful contacts, although their knowledge of Russia may be limited:

RADAR The principal UK forum and pressure group for people with disabilities. ⓐ 12 City Forum, 250 City Road, London EC1V 8AF ⓣ 0207 250 3222 ⓦ www.radar.org.uk

SATH (Society for Accessible Travel & Hospitality) Advises US-based travellers with disabilities. ⓐ 347 Fifth Ave, Suite 610, New York, NY 10016 ⓣ 212 447 7284 ⓦ www.sath.org

TOURIST INFORMATION

Despite its relative popularity as a city break destination, Moscow has no tourist information office. Most visitors fall back on their hotel lobby or tour company for info and the internet is also a useful resource. Russia does run a network of tourist offices abroad but these are of limited use and seem to operate more as visa and tour agencies.

Russian National Tourist Offices

London ⓐ 70 Piccadilly, London W1J 8HP ⓣ (020) 7495 7570 ⓦ www.visitrussia.org.uk

Edinburgh ⓐ 16 Forth Street, Edinburgh EH1 3LH ⓣ (0131) 550 3709 ⓦ www.visitrussia.org.uk

New York ⓐ 224 West 30th Street, suite 701, New York, NY 10001 ⓣ 877 221 7120 ⓦ www.russia-travel.com

BACKGROUND READING

Dr Zhivago by Boris Pasternak. Much of the early action takes place in Moscow.

Gorky Park; Polar Star, Red Square by Martin Cruz Smith. Detective thrillers set in 1980s and 1990s Moscow.

Inside Putin's Russia by Jack Andrew. An account of former President Putin's first term in office.

The Master and Margarita by Mikhail Bulgakov. A Russian classic set in Moscow.

Ten Days that Shook the World by John Reed. An eyewitness account of the 1917 Bolshevik revolution.

Emergencies

The following are emergency free-call numbers:
Ambulance 03
Fire 01
Police 02
Emergency (in English) (495) 937 9911

MEDICAL SERVICES

Before travelling to Moscow, it is well worth making sure you have full medical insurance valid in the Russian Federation. Should you be unfortunate enough to have a medical problem while in Moscow, you are advised to use private medical facilities where English is spoken, as Russian public healthcare facilities are dire.

American Medical Center Grokholsky per. 1 (495) 933 7700 www.amcenters.com 24 hrs Metro: Prospekt Mira

EMERGENCY PHRASES

Fire!	**Help!**	**Stop!**
Пожар!	Помогите!	Прекратите!
Pa-zhar!	*Pa-ma-gi-tye!*	*Pri-kra-ti-tye!*

Call a doctor/the police/an ambulance!
Вызовите врача/милицию/скорую!
Vih-za-vit-ye vra-cha/mi-lit-sih-yu/sko-ru-yu!

European Dental Centre ⓐ 1st Nikoloschepovsky per. 6/1 ⓣ (495) 933 0002 ⓦ www.emcmos.ru ⓛ 09.00–21.00 Mon–Fri, 09.00–20.00 Sat & Sun ⓜ Metro: Smolenskaya

European Medical Centre ⓐ Spiridonievsky per. 5/1 ⓣ (495) 933 6655 ⓦ www.emcmos.ru ⓛ 24 hrs ⓜ Metro: Mayakovskaya or Pushkinskaya

POLICE

Although things have improved in recent years, the Russian police (*Militsiya*) are probably best avoided unless you run into really serious trouble. If you are robbed, you'll need to go to a police post or station to get a report for your insurance company. There is a *Militsiya* post at every metro station.

EMBASSIES & CONSULATES

Australia ⓐ Podkolokolny per. 10A/2 ⓣ (495) 956 6070 ⓦ www.russia.embassy.gov.au ⓜ Metro: Kitay-Gorod

Canada ⓐ Starokonyushenny per. 23 ⓣ (495) 925 6000 ⓦ www.dfait-maeci.gc.ca ⓜ Metro: Kropotkinskaya

South Africa ⓐ Granatny per. 1/9 ⓣ (495) 926 1177 ⓦ www.saembassy.ru ⓜ Metro: Arbatskaya

USA ⓐ Bolshoy Devyatinsky per. 8 ⓣ (495) 728 5000 ⓦ http://moscow.usembassy.gov ⓜ Metro: Barrikadnaya

UK ⓐ Smolenskaya Naberezhnaya 10 ⓣ (495) 956 7200 ⓦ http://ukinrussia.fco.gov.uk ⓜ Metro: Smolenskaya

Editorial/project management: Lisa Plumridge
Copy editor: Monica Guy
Layout/DTP: Alison Rayner

The publishers would like to thank the following individuals and organisations for supplying their copyright photographs for this book: 123RF.com (Astroid, page 99; Denis Babenko, pages 45 & 73; Galina Barskaya, page 5; Alexey Fateev, page 38; Vladimir Fedoroff, page 57; Mikhail Morozov, page 21; Elena Morozova, page 93; Pavel Parmenov, page 79); Marc Di Duca, pages 13, 15, 61, 83 & 133; Dreamstime.com (Alexander Avdeev, pages 7, 107 & 113; Atanas Bozhikov, page 24; Sergey Danilin, page 119; Alexey Efanov, page 8; Inta Eihmane, page 96; Vladimir Georgievsky, page 127; Igor Kharlamov, page 70; Alexey Khromushin, page 116; Pavel Losevsky, pages 17,

Send your thoughts to
books@thomascook.com

- **Found a great bar, club, shop or must-see sight that we don't feature?**
- **Like to tip us off about any information that needs a little updating?**
- **Want to tell us what you love about this handy little guidebook and more importantly how we can make it even handier?**

Then here's your chance to tell all! Send us ideas, discoveries and recommendations today and then look out for your valuable input in the next edition of this title.

Email the above address (stating the title) or write to:
pocket guides Series Editor, Thomas Cook Publishing, PO Box 227, Coningsby Road, Peterborough PE3 8SB, UK.

WHAT'S IN YOUR GUIDEBOOK?

Independent authors Impartial up-to-date information from our travel experts who meticulously source local knowledge.

Experience Thomas Cook's 165 years in the travel industry and guidebook publishing enriches every word with expertise you can trust.

Travel know-how Thomas Cook has thousands of staff working around the globe, all living and breathing travel.

Editors Travel-publishing professionals, pulling everything together to craft a perfect blend of words, pictures, maps and design.

You, the traveller We deliver a practical, no-nonsense approach to information, geared to how you really use it.

18–19, 20, 23, 31 & 52; Vladimir Melnik, page 111; Alena Ozerova, page 27; Vladimir Salazkin, page 35; Julia Shepeleva, page 47; Elena Solodovnikova, page 123; Sunlu4ik, page 105; Vadim Zholobov, page 32); Godunov, page 76; NOVIKOV Group, page 90; Punxutawneyphil, page 125; SXC.hu (Matthijs Mejan, pages 40–1 & 59; Yaroslav Ushakov, pages 43 & 69), Karen Yee, page 87.

Useful phrases

English	Russian	*Approx pronunciation*
BASICS		
Yes	Да	*Da*
No	Нет	*Nyet*
Please	Пожалуйста	*Pa-zhal-sta*
Thank you	Спасибо	*Spa-si-ba*
Hello	Здравствуйте	*Zdrast-vuyt-ye*
Goodbye	До свидания	*Da svi-dan-ya*
Excuse me (to get past)	Разрешите	*Raz-ri-shiht-ye*
Excuse me (attention/apology)	Извините	*Iz-vi-nit-ye*
I don't speak Russian	Я не говорю по-русски	*Ya nye ga-var-yu pa-ru-ski*
Do you speak English?	Вы говорите по-английски?	*Vih ga-va-rit-ye pa-an-gli-ski?*
Good morning	Доброе утро	*Do-bra-ye u-tra*
Good afternoon	Добрый день	*Do-brih dyen*
Good evening	Добрый вечер	*Do-brih vye-chir*
Goodnight	Спокойной ночи	*Spa-koy-ney no-chi*
My name is ...	Меня зовут ...	*Min-ya za-vut ...*
NUMBERS		
One	Один/Одна/Одно (m/f/n)	*A-din/Ad-na/Ad-no*
Two	Два/Две (m & n/f)	*Dva/Dvye*
Three	Три	*Tri*
Four	Четыре	*Chi-tih-ri*
Five	Пять	*Pyat*
Six	Шесть	*Shest*
Seven	Семь	*System*
Eight	Восемь	*Vo-sim*
Nine	Девять	*Dye-vit*
Ten	Десять	*Dye-sit*
Eleven	Одиннадцать	*A-di-nat-sat*
Twelve	Двенадцать	*Dvi-nat-sat*
Twenty	Двадцать	*Dvat-sat*
Fifty	Пятьдесят	*Pi-dis-yat*
One hundred	Сто	*Sto*
One thousand	Тысяча	*Tih-si-cha*
SIGNS & NOTICES		
Airport	Аэропорт	*A-e-ra-port*
Rail station	Вокзал (m)	*Vag-zal*
Platform	Платформа (f)	*Plat-for-ma*
Smoking/non-smoking	Для курящих/ Не курить	*D-lya kou-rya-sch-ikh/ Neh ku-rit*
Toilets	Туалет (m)	*Tu-al-yet*
Ladies/Gentlemen	Ж/М	
Subway (train)	Метро (n)	*Mi-tro*